SOCIOECONOMIC DISADVANTAGE

AND

POVERTY IN POLYGYNY AFRICAN FAMILIES

I0172715

Majok Wutchok

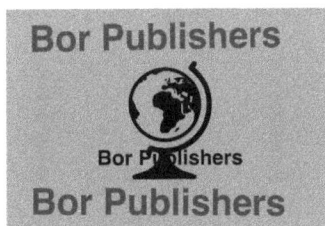

Bor Publishers

Bor Publishers

Bor Publishers

Bor Publishers

DEDICATION

This book is purposely dedicated to my daughter Achol, my two boys Kur, De'Von Deng, my younger siblings and my own special, Eunice.

Table of Contents

PREFACE

This book titled *"Socioeconomic Disadvantage and Poverty in Polygyny African Families"* unambiguously deliberates on several challenges faced mainly by large families peculiar to several African countries. Asides the issue of poverty and lack of funds to take care of the large families, this book further talks about the misconceptions and lack of adequate information and knowledge towards child bearing and family planning in general. Also, the misconceptions about gender equality in children as well as the huge expectations placed on the girl child at a tender age towards early child marriage. It is quite unfortunate that most illiterate parents who tend to bear more children they can't cater for, often depends on government, foreign aid and also charitable organizations to help take care of their children. Acts like this has painted Africa as a continent that lacks resources and depends directly or indirectly on grants and aids from humanitarian agencies.

Africa, a continent rich with surplus natural and human resources as well as great ecological, economic and cultural diversity, yet still underdeveloped. Most African countries have suffered and are still suffering from corruption, military and monarch dictatorship, deep poverty, war and civil unrest. Majority of the nations UN classified as least developed are predominantly in Africa. Several development strategies have been adopted and have proven abortive to the yielding of expected results. Even though some individual are of the opinion Africa is cursed to remain in perpetual economic slavery and poverty, Africa is a continent with great potential.

The mitigation of poverty in large African families can be achievable via adopting the knowledge of family planning and the acceptance of birth control. However, the religious and cultural perspective towards having large families counters the acceptance and application of family planning knowledge, that is, traditional tribes in African countries believes it is the right of the patriarchy to determine the number of spouses (wife) and offspring to have in an household, therefore disregarding the knowledge of family planning as a taboo or abomination to their culture or religion. In the ancient times of some West African countries, particularly Nigeria, a ruler or an affluent man can have more than 6 wives, some parts are reportedly to have 20 wives or more and bear more children they are unable to cater for emotionally as a father even if they are well to-do financially. Asides being affluent, the provision of amenities by the government, economic and market failure may potentially affect these families and results into several shortcomings towards child development.

Evidently, extreme poverty will result into stunted development as an adult as well as limited productivity in the nearest future thereby leading to the continuous passing down of intergenerational poverty. The coping mechanism of adult parents is far wide different from that of children in extreme poverty, and peculiar to some African countries that live on less than $2 per day. Extreme poverty faced by large African families is liable to result into high mortality rate or ruin individual's potential in the nearest future. The total number of young ones in abject poverty points to the actual need to invest specifically in the primary years especially in quality education, clean water pre-natal and ante-natal care for pregnant mothers, good sanitation, early childhood development programs as well as universal healthcare. Refining these services as well as ensuring that current African childhood can way in into quality job opportunities when the time comes as the only way to disrupt and destroy the cycle of intergenerational deficiency that is common in Africa today.

Sub-Saharan Africa does not only have highest fraction of children living in abject poverty, it accounts for the great share of the world's awfully poor children, Malnourishment and related health issues in children is one of the most revealing signs of extreme poverty where about 25% of offspring under age of 5 years old appear to be too short and short for their age. The rural areas in Africa are predominantly found to four times more likely live in abject poverty than those living in civilized urban parts of the African country. However, kids living in households with higher incomes are strangely affected by poverty.

African countries affected by poor economic administration, conflict, political instability are likely to have increased number of children living below $2 per day. This increases the risk of malnutrition, inadequate healthcare and education thereby making them highly susceptible to different kinds of child abuse and exploitation. Foreign aids calls the attention of the government of every African country to include children in poverty alleviation plans as a matter of urgency as well as confirm that extreme poverty of children is more often than not measured and attended to at national levels. Thoughtful child social defence systems like cash transfer programs that pay up families directly are helpful in eliminating abject poverty amongst children.

The high mortality rates of children in Africa contributes immensely to larger African families, as illiterate parents tend to give birth to more children so as to cover up for the loss of any offspring. Other challenges faced by low income African elders are categorized into three which includes a.) Elders are looked up to cater and take up responsibilities of the family as they are the major providers and caregiver to their children, b.) The problem on the elders has increased with the high rate of mortality amongst teenagers in their prime due regional conflicts and increased pandemic rates of HIV-AIDS, c.) The customary safety net of the extended family has been rendered ineffective and undependable for the elderly. Even though some number of researches has studied the welfare consequences of these developments on children. Some research have analysed the poverty situation amongst elderly groups systematically in Africa especially low-income countries as well as role of social pensions.

As stated by an expert, Dr. Singh, Development and Education are the best contraceptive for African couples living in rural areas. Although limited access to contraception also poses a great challenge, however, the acceptance and adaptation of the use of contraceptive is essential. The engaging of women in formal education in rural areas and well as urban parts of some African countries with low GDP will reduce significantly the rate of child conception. Improving the female child participation in school will overtime lower the rate of fertility, it is discovered that the more the years a girl child uses in schooling the more time it delays the conception of her first child by 10 to 12 months. Educating the girl child will help older women skilfully put limitation towards the number of children intended to conceive.

The most pressured and susceptible individual in a poverty stricken large family in Africa is the girl child, asides being burdened with huge expectation that surpasses their age, they are vulnerable to abuse and other forms of child molestation and exploitation, example of which is early child marriage. This has led to several health related issues and misconceptions and worse death in the past as the girl child is yet to be fully matured to go through the rigorous process of a wife and motherhood at such a tender age. Asides that, the girl child is not provided with adequate healthcare system to support or give immediate post-natal care as well as hygienic which may cause complications for the mother or the newborn and may unfortunately result into death. The life of an average Sub-Saharan African girl child especially in South

Sudan, Northern Uganda, Northern and Western Kenya, part of Ethiopia, rural Tanzania, some part of Malawi, DRC, some West African countries and Northern Nigeria is strangely complex especially when born into a large poor family. As young as the age of 10 are betrothed to a matured male and after reaching the puberty stage, she is ceremoniously led to her betrothed husband house to resume wife and mother duties at a young age.

The gender-learning gap is prevalent in Sub-Saharan Africa especially in rural areas, the kind of education they are exposed to especially the girl child is not as authentic as the learning of critical formal skills such as numeracy or calculative math reading and writing. In view of the impact of rural poverty across Africa, the rural areas school children in most African countries are at a disadvantage pace when it comes to the provision of quality education judging from a socioeconomic point of view. Generally, the rural areas have less teachers who are less qualified for the number of enrolled children which evidently points out the low qualified teachers-per-school i.e. 100 pupils to one teacher. The causes of low numbers of qualified teachers are many and also complex some of which are linked to socioeconomic conditions, inequalities and poverty. For instance, teachers naturally opt for urban areas than rural areas schools because of huge opportunities and prospects in the urban areas and most importantly higher income. Also, there is better life quality in urban areas not to be compared to that in rural areas such as access to quality infrastructure, general public amenities and other services.

UNICEF identifies the major barriers affecting quality education in rural areas of some African countries that is as a result of poverty and instability. They include;

- Crisis and Instability,

- Direct and indirect costs (i.e. feeding, clothing, and cost of attending school),

- Poor quality processes (lack of quality infrastructure and qualified teachers in rural areas),

- Health and Nutrition,

- Traditional practices,

- Lack of nation's budgetary to education,

- Poor quality content (obsolete learning curriculum),

- Distance to school, etc.

These barriers prevalently affect children in conflicted areas, the female child, children with disabilities, children from large poor families, children from minority ethnic groups. These groups of kids are further at disadvantaged pace due to the lack of education to their parents. The improving of health care centres and sanitation conditions will help reduce the drastic drop out of school children due to strange illnesses. The improving of quality agricultural sector in rural areas will in turn result into a more comfortable life for parents and children with large families living on minute income per day, it saves the child, mother and father from malnutrition and hunger related issues. A hungry man is an angry man they say; a hungry child is an uninterested child in education. To curb out long term intergenerational passing down of poverty, it is therefore imperative for government of low-income African countries to invest in quality education and general stable life of rural areas so as to significantly reduce the learning gap between children living in rural areas and urban areas.

Subsequent chapters of this book highlights the concepts and misconceptions that are linked to cultural and religious beliefs towards large poor African families and the adamant refusal to adopt family planning. Also, the issue of domestic violence in child, women and men in different cultural views are explicitly discussed in this book. The basic concept as regards dowry, wife ownership and major causes of financial mistrust and complications in marriages are also addressed in this book alongside different ways to curb or salvage the marriage. Moreover, the role of parents in the empowerment and engagement of their children cannot be overemphasized as they easily influence their kids whom mirror their character and attitude towards work.

Majok Wutchok,

Perth, Western Australia

April 2018.

Books published by Majok Wutchok.

Unimaginatively Western World! (What makes immigrants parents struggle raising their children in western world) Short book, 2018.

Introduction to County Public Health Strategic Plan (County Level, South Sudan). Guideline book, 2018.

CHAPTER 1

ECONOMIC AND GOVERNMENT FAILURE

The impact of economic and governmental administration failure cannot be overemphasized as it has characterized Africa as a continent that constantly seeks foreign aid support and saddled with the burden of child poverty. Corruption being a major factor that causes immense failure of socioeconomic development is the order of the day has its adverse effect on larger African families especially people living in the rural areas. Poverty effects are deeply and complexly connected to large monogamy and polygamy African families. On the other hand, it is useful to identify individually the cause and effects of poverty before discerning them in relation to one effect or another. Also, it will help identify major causes of poverty well to know how to eliminate poverty totally. The main effects and implications of poverty are explicitly discussed in this chapter as well as ways to help alleviate poverty in many African nations either low-income or high-income countries.

Evidently, most African countries are developing countries and will be unfair to measure poverty the same way one would with a developed country. Also, the lifestyle of a developed country does not warrant having extended polygamy family, in most developed countries, families are most nuclear, one man one wife. Although there is no direct link that relates economic growth with poverty, but the important part is the institutions that manage the society, also the impact of economic failure depends greatly on the nation's inequalities of the nation's prevailing economy. The economy of a nation can be affected by poverty in several ways. Poverty affects the economy of a country when funds and budget needed to fund the supply-chain for producing; distributing, selling and revenue generation is diverted to the creation of programs to assist unemployment payments, poverty alleviation programs, welfare programs and management. The funds allocated to these programs are used to salvage and initiate welfare programs, where it can be pumped into producing and generating capital and funds to the country's economy.

The quality of life and improvement of lifestyle in large African families are faced with risks and vulnerability especially families living in rural areas of low-income countries who largely depend on tropical and agricultural ecosystems. Some factors that contributes to the vulnerabilities and risks that contribute and drive poverty includes conflicts and market failure. Market failure otherwise known as economic failure and market instability increase the frequency of poverty in Africa. In addition, when the resources or facility intended for 200 capacity is used and overworked by 2000 people, it is expected to breakdown and increase the hardship faced by the people who are in urgent need of such resource or faculty.

Complications and consequences of economic and market failure on large African families increase the rate of conflict, as it is expected to experience 'survival of the fittest' and hoarding of resources for use. Some preferential treatment comes into place and thereby results into bribery and corruption popularly referred to as 'by-passing the system' or kitu kidogo in East Africa. These acts further enrich the rich and render the poor even poorer; this is one of the main causes of immigration of African migrants to other countries for search of greener pastures and better opportunities. In addition to this, the percentage of the rich in most African countries exploited the riches in Africa particularly those in government that embezzled and exports these funds into foreign countries and enriched their families like the case of South Sudan aristocracy.

The poor families in the sub-Saharan Africa lack the level of assets either human capital or physical assets essential to guard themselves against shocks from market instability and economic failure. The insufficient infrastructural and institutional linkages such as roads, railways, mobile telecommunication etc. amidst local and international markets that explains the markets are badly integrated over the space and time. The charges of fast population growth are increasing, that is more conception today renders the work of reducing population growth in the future difficult as the younger ones of today are the parents of tomorrow. Generally, agricultural production and food supplies need to be increased greatly to meet the needs of increased growing population which limits the allocation of resources to other socioeconomic sectors of the country.

The mental and physical developments of children in large families are somehow frequently poor due to malnutrition and little or no parental supervision at a young and tender age through to the adolescent stage of the child. The dominance of diseases related to poverty and malnutrition are also contributing factors.

Moreover, the fast increase in population implies that there will be an upsurge in dependency ratio which means that the nation affected will have to budget funds to educate and provide general welfare for the population that only consume but does not produce or adds to the economy of the country positively. Also, the large African families have serious consequences for the provision of prolific and industrious employment positions since it is known that high population rate is usually linked with increase in labour force. This implies that the rate of job creation should equal the rate of supply of workforce. In most African countries, the supply of workforce has outweighed the supply of available job, which means that the rate of unemployment has upsurge, implying that qualified job seekers are twenty times more than the available job, which contributes to the ominous challenges of the society.

In the case of ever-increasing number of labour that cannot be fully engaged into the modern socioeconomic sectors of several African countries, these human capital or assets are either forced back into traditional section with low wage ad low productivity or unproductive quack service occupations. The availability of cheap and dispensable labour tends to pull back the industrialization and technological change, which in turn is greatly delayed by poverty and the call for manufactured goods is reduced. Consequentially, this results into reduced quality of skilled labour and low savings rate of the nation, which hinder the total development and application of the natural resources in certain African countries. The increasing populations outpace the rate at which renewable resources can be sustained; there is a great likelihood for such resources to be expended. Therefore, the international trade of certain African nations can be distorted or degraded due to low efficiency of labour and its productivity, poverty and the slow industrialization with increasing rate of demand for food and basic human necessities.

In urban areas, most young educated millennial who may or may not be from large families depends greatly on gig economy as a side job or way to survive the present hardship of unemployment. Painting bad image of the country, fraudulent acts are rampant amongst youths in some African countries, looking for quick ways to get wealth and engaging in online and offline dubious activities and end up squandering it or getting caught in the act. The crime rates and the use and abuse of drugs skyrockets, in addition to these, there is a high rate of teenage pregnancy further contributing to population growth and increasing the rates of poverty alleviation.

In urban areas of African countries, poor large families who moved to the cities contributes to the development of slums and ghettos as housing facilities are not provided or projected for the current population. The development of slums further leads to social problems where gangs, crimes and bad sanitation is common. Reduced housing facilities, overcrowded basic amenities, increased unemployment and increased population growth will always put the country's budget at jeopardy instead of producing goods and services for positive economic impact, it is used to organize welfare programs. However, these allocated funds are not duly accounted for and at greater risks of embezzlement by officials to western nations.

Increased population growth as a result of indiscriminate and uncontrolled conception of most large families in Africa have difficulties for social and political conflicts amongst the different kinds of social, religious, cultural and linguistic groups. As expected, there will be increasing demands of services in education, sanitation, healthcare and other function. Riots and violent aggression erupts especially from younger people who are unemployed and have little or no hope of a comfortable prospective future. The cost and nature of welfare and health services may be jeopardized by fast population growth Just as much as that of formal education services. Rate of illness and death occurrences in families may be on the high side due to the increased rate of fertility and recurrent pregnancies as well as the need for caring for too many children at the same time.

Furthermore, the agricultural lands of large African families are not permitted to lay fallow for longer periods thereby enacting lots of pressure on the soil, the land set aside for grazing experiences overgrazing, this causes a potential conflict between herders and farmers. In Western Africa for instance, there has been a major issue breeding conflicts resulting into the loss of life and property on a large scale where herders move from the overgrazed into farmlands and destroy the farm produce. Therefore, increased population growth has not only influenced poverty on a large scaled but also put the security of life and property at jeopardy.

CHAPTER 2

ILLITERACY

Education they say is one of the most potent weapons that can be used to impact change to the world positively. Today, education is essential to human development to be able to adopt and thrive in the knowledge and technological advanced world of today. Illiteracy places Africa at the bottom of the technological advanced world, as the level of quality education is on the lacking side of most African countries, there are no new changes to the out-dated curriculum thereby causing a slow paced development. Often referred as a continent with 90% developing countries, Africans plagued with illiteracy at a damning level, this pace has further promoted superstitious beliefs. The disease of social development is what illiteracy is, as it puts the growth and development of a community in jeopardy.

In developing countries of Africa, millions of children are out of school and are left with below par knowledge of basic communication (i.e. reading, writing and speaking), formal logical reasoning and calculative forms (math) of formal education that may influence the productivity of the country's economy. Contented with crude and traditional agricultural skills, education is not particularly welcomed in rural areas of Africa particularly for those of larger families as it is believed the larger family provides a large human workforce and the time spent within the shores of a classroom reduce the productivity of farming.

A large percentage circa 90% of all illiterate people in the world reside in developing countries to which 70% are women, that means the rate of female illiteracy in Africa is on a high side especially in Sub-Saharan Africa. For instances, in South Sudan and Burkina Faso over 98% and 90% respectively of the women of these countries are illiterate, this influences the rate of population growth and early marriages and conception, and it also determines life expectancy of the female. In the education market, the rapid population growth contributes to the imbalance of the world's educational development towards moving towards a progressive direction.

Almost a billion people were discovered to be illiterate in the year 2000, to which 2 out of 3 were women, female illiteracy will adversely affect the possibilities to obtain a job as well as contribute to other economic and social variables like nutrition and well being as well as likelihood to run a company. 70% of women of the world's developing countries are illiterate, Africa as a continent has a high level of illiteracy than the rest of the world. Mali, Niger and Burkina Faso are countries with the worst case of illiteracy in the dessert, about 90% of the adult female populace were discovered to be uneducated in 2005 which was a result of low school enrolment, low quality of formal education, poverty and rapid growth of population.

Also, illiteracy poses a strong force against the introduction, acceptance and application of medical recommendations as regards controlling of rapid population growth. For instance, an uneducated man at an old age with more than three wives and twelve kids will see the possibility of marrying more wives and having more kids because of superstitious beliefs and cultural acceptance. Asides, population growth and poverty, the health of the wives and kids are at risk, as there are inherent illnesses such as the pandemic HIV-AIDS that plagues Africa. The linguistic framework affects the environment of education in Africa, the teachings are given in a foreign language to which the students are not used to, and also it is taught in language the teacher does not fully comprehend.

Policies that support the educational sector should be brought up; examples are the provision of written materials in native languages that give huge returns in terms of encouraging literacy. African languages in formal education should be supported especially in basic primary schools, as language of instructions dedicated to support easy and fast comprehension for pupils at young age. Linguistic barrier poses a huge threat to the educational planning and development of the continent; each country in Africa has more than one particular tribe. For instance, in South Sudan, there are four major tribes namely Dinka, Nuer, Bari, Zande and within these tribes there are ethnic minority groups that speaks different languages, in total there are over 64 ethnic minority groups in South Sudan, however, the language of the four major tribes can best be spoken and understood in classes.

Education should be encouraged in the native tongue of the tribal lingua franca as well as the urban language thereby making the four-language formulas become a customary practice in several schools in the developing country. In addition, the allegory about the vast diversity of language in Africa is untrue, because a total of 85% of Africans speak up to 12 to 15 major languages to which they are often comparable to each other than the imposed colonial languages. Intergenerational transmission of illiteracy is immense in Africa, the possibilities of poverty being prominent especially in larger families is high, because there is zero encouragement as regards schooling from parents and little books are made available at home to stimulate reading at home.

Also, since the parents are with little or no schooling, it is expected for children to be withdrawn or dropout from schools either because of lack of funds or lack of interest. Besides, in poor households especially in larger families, surviving is more prioritized as it is a constant challenge experienced on a daily basis, therefore children are out of school to work to support their parents especially in cases of extreme poverty. Therefore, children contribute to the income of the family however making it difficult to give preference to schooling as poverty as well as other limitation is luxuries poor parents cannot afford for their children.

It has been discovered that rapid population growth is closely related with the number of offspring per woman in developing countries where the basic school enrolment for the female child is high; it leads to a significant reduction in child mortality. The rate of fertility is also negatively related with the number of female child registered in basic school, indicating that education of women is a very important factor in the clarification of the fertility tendency perceived in African countries. Also, it constitutes to a significant variable of the link amidst demographic growth and development. Auspiciously, it is convincing the evidence of the importance of encouraging education to attain development.

Logical distribution of education associates with lower rate of economic poverty as well as inequality and rapid economic growth. Literacy for girls has progressive impacts on women's empowerment and reduced the risk of women's poverty. Indirect benefits are generated as well in terms of family nutrition, health of the newborn and children, immunization and rate of education for their children. According to various researchers, it has been discovered that male and female children living in Sub-Saharan African countries may be the lasting effective nuclear head against the endemic HIV/AIDS. Basic education similarly contributes to improved management of natural resources. Also, secondary and tertiary education levels are basic for globally competitive economies and building of democratic communities.

African parents who are aged 50 and above with low level of literacy have the peculiarity of belonging to the age groups for whom there were eye-catching job opportunities despite their level of education. A significant number of them have never felt the urge or the logic behind going back to school for self-development, because they have over a long period of time, married and started their family on the same job, it makes further education an illogical attempt to them. Unfortunately, the closing down of these companies especially primary and manufacturing sectors, due to the revolution of technological advancements e.g. there are no needs for phonebooks, and everyone can access their contacts via email or other social media platforms to access their contacts. Many are out of job and add to the population of the unemployed family looking up to a financially unstable breadwinner, in the bid not to starve to death, children are withdrawn from school and enrolled into some cheap skill acquisition centres. It is quite difficult securing a job again because of the difficulty in writing, reading and comprehension of the new forms of economy the country has introduced due to civilization and urban advancement. Besides, the lack of skill set requires meeting up with the present market and political requirements or to register in training would hinder their possibility of being qualified.

In summary, literacy is a potent instrument for lowering inequality and poverty as well as laying foundations for sustainable growth of economy, sound governance and effective institutions. In spite of improvements in the universal basic education admissions, countries in Sub-Saharan Africa are still faced with several education problems. Less than 60% of adults in developing countries on the average can write and read with comprehension. Although there are several reasons the level of literacy in Africa is low, for example Africa happens to have many teenagers between the age of 13 to 15, thereby making it quite a bit of a challenge for governments to enable education for teenagers because of the ever-increasing number of students within a very limited national budget.

CHAPTER 3

RELIGION AND CULTURAL PERSPECTIVE ON LARGE FAMILIES.

Cultural and religious beliefs of large African families is a very strong one, especially the Islamic religion where it is believed that a man has the rights to marry more than two wives but at most four wives provided he has the means to provide and cater for them accordingly without disputes. Also, according to ancient traditional practices, large families are a norm to which the ancestors accept its occurrence and multiplication. However, the rights and autonomy of each person should be enjoyed in the marriage relationship. Large families in Africa are as a unit of reproduction, accumulation, production and consumption, which have been deeply impacted by the downturn of the country's economy that transformed the immediate environment, which also influences how the family come about their decisions. These wider economic and socio-political environments avail the contexts for understanding changes in the family structures of Africa.

Projections have arisen from significant socioeconomic modifications that continue to modify the structure of the family unit away from old-fashioned customary structures to new ones generated by the development of healthcare systems, education, migration and employment. However, the same forces that produce important scenes for families have resulted into the outcome of diverse constraints. African large families are embedded in socioeconomic and political situations that are categorized as long-lasting domestic dynamics of fragility, poor governance, civil conflicts and incapacitating poverty. All through the 1990s, the plague of the pandemic HIV/AIDS has led to extra pressure on the sustainability of households and large families. Likewise, the novel demands released by the forces of civilization and globalization have had mixed outcomes for African families, concurrently improving the opportunities to grab the chances for inclusion in great economic exchanges, despite the fact that at the same increasing their susceptibility and variability to these forces. Therefore, the condition and position of African families is clouded by the challenging strains of economic and social regeneration constraints.

Typically, a native African man is religious to the core and proud of his roots, also human relation and religion to an African man shows that religion is indeed a social function. As stimulus and morals are basic fundamentals of cultural environment, which for that reason society based. Therefore, marital relationship to any African goes beyond interpersonal and intra-personal to accept supernatural beings or when it involves elements, processes or abilities, which are superhuman and would easily pass as an extra-mundane relationship. Too concerned about the morality of the female, especially the rural Muslims in the western parts of Africa, the female child is married off at an early age contributing to early marriage and increasing the rate of child mortality as well as rapid spread of the endemic HIV/AIDS in younger generation. Also, for the continuity of a particular clan, larger families are encouraged to further increase the number of descendants of that particular clan.

The high fertility rate of most African families even with the advent of civilization and modernization still baffles most researchers. Most assumptions are placed on the cultural and traditional role and its contribution to increased fertility rate, however it is almost not compatible with reasoning proper to a contemporary social setting that favours a community based on nuclear families and individuals rather than kinship or large families. Comparatively, the fact that urban and civilized individuals in urban settings of developing countries in Africa have to segregate their lives between work and family, between colleagues and relation, depicts that they are unable to regard themselves as fitting merely into a single social group. Evidently, they live their lives in several social contexts, which are somehow induced to explain a personal synthesis of the efforts they receive in each of these social contexts. A blend that improve their self-conscience as individual spiritual beings and not just as members of a mere social group that permeates all the scopes of their lives. Therefore, staying true to their ancient cultural beliefs and way of life will be as a result of personal decisions and not as a result of compulsion or necessities.

Taking a look at the affiliations between large family's fertility rate and religion as it contributes or links to poverty via dynamic and lifetime views as well as employing a quality nuanced and contextualized classification of religious (Christianity) denominational variety than most studies on fertility and religion typical use. The denominational differences associations were due to characteristic perspective in age, urban background and exposure, marriage experience, and education.

Religion especially the Islamic religion has its own way of controlling the rate of fertility and pregnancy in the continent, i.e. during the period of Ramadan, either civilized or uneducated Muslims keeps themselves consecrated and abstain from lovemaking for a whole month to be fully fortified for the blessings of the Supreme Being. This reduces the rate of fertility and conception rate in the continent. In the same vein, Christian religious fanatics believe that consecration of one's body is the ultimate worship to the Supreme Being and everything including child bearing should be done with utmost moderation. However, due to lack of quality education in most rural parts of the continent, the ancient culture of child bearing is followed to the latter amidst other factors that hinders the proper taking care of such large family.

Conclusively, the impact of religious and cultural perspective on fertility and its link to poverty cannot be over stressed as the negative impact of socio-political differences has prompted insufficiency and corruption in the institutions to be enjoyed by the masses. Also, any typical African is proud of their roots either educated and or influential, the need to have a larger family is majorly based on personal decisions. For instance, the Islamic religion embraces polygyny and large families while Christianity preaches moderations; therefore despite the advent of education, personal decision is very key to the continuity of larger families. In addition, the continuity of any ethnic minority is prioritized.

CHAPTER 4

ROLE OF POLYGYNY IN AFRICAN HOMES.

Preceding the arrival of Christianity and colonialism, polygyny is widely practiced in Africa, as it signifies the aspect of culture. More reason polygyny is prevalent in African homes is due to the fact that children are considered as a form of wealth by the society and a larger family is considered influential and powerful. Therefore this practice was deliberated as one of the way one could build an empire in Africa. It was after the era of colonialism in Africa that polygamy appeared to be a taboo as it was a norm in ancient times. Polygyny has been linked to the positive (the hustling and survival of the fittest spirit already instilled) and negative causes of child survival, but in general, high mortality and poor health are well experienced in polygamous families. Comparatively, children from nuclear families are not vulnerable to the risk of mortality and nutritional deficiency before the age of five like children from polygamous families.

Polygyny signifies a peculiar cultural approach to marriage, reproduction and family and not just a single-family structure unit.

There is a huge difference in the prevalence of the practice of polygamy both within and between the Sub-Saharan region countries of Africa. Situations in which polygyny is prevalent and tends to be socially, culturally and economically different from those in which such practice is uncommon. For instance, polygyny is most popular in rural contexts and in some urban context as well. Away from these socioeconomic alterations, extensive polygyny also reflects a separate set of cultural traditions, which are obvious in the distinctive demographic forms and gender standards that depicts highly polygamous situations.

The unique social, economic and cultural attributes of extremely polygamous settings opines that away from the implication for the families that engage in it, the contextual dominance of polygyny may be significant to comprehending the patterns of newborn mortality in Sub-Saharan Africa. The prevalence of polygyny could be linked with newborn mortality falsely, via its connection with socioeconomic disadvantage. Consecutively, the shared knowledge of living in an environment where polygyny is culturally standardized reflecting well-known gender inequality may result to an uninterrupted association with infant mortality. Also, since polygamy in extreme polygamous environment is economically and socially unique from polygamy where it is uncommon, it may alter the survival disadvantage related with living in a polygamous family.

Oftentimes, undue emphasis is placed on sexuality when deliberating on polygyny; also it achieves the peculiar function that is secluded to describing the sexual gender of a man. Overgeneralized, polygyny improves production in rural parts of Africa in the sense that the larger the family the wider the portion of land allocated to be cultivated. In addition, it makes livestock rearing and food organization simpler and better organized thereby resulting in improved food production. There are other delicate purposes such as the symbolism of bearing many children, the display of affluence and in some contexts just complying with cultural beliefs. It is imperative to know that no human practice is an exception to abuse, however due to personal decisions people with reasons best known to them can abuse some practices which may not be lawful.

Polygamy is rendered useless when individuals only engage in polygamy just to exploit the sexual perks of having more than one partner. However, the sexual benefits are not the main functions, polygyny is reducing in Africa not as a result of the intervention of westernization but for the varying economy and the general usual cultural climate. Customarily, most African communities have experienced a custom polygamy. Prior to the arrival of Christianity in Africa, polygamy was not considered evil, the custom permits a man to marry as many spouse as he can cater and support, they are married agreeing to local customs and legitimate in the comprehension of local world-view.

Below are some of the reasons why polygyny is valued and practiced in Africa, they include;

- A man's affluence is determined by the number of significant other and number of offspring as well as livestock he has in his possession.

- In political terms, the more the spouses a man has, the more political associations that can be formed and therefor become an effective chief, tribal leader, political figure or king.

- In agrarian societies, human capital i.e. workforce is important and therefore polygyny provided more effective efforts to work on the fields and produce more food for consumption and for sale. Therefore, polygamy generated affluence for the head of household.

- During the old times, it was honourable and respected to have many wives especially a community ruler.

- Strangely, polygyny availed a form of birth control to which spacing of children is permitted by virtue of the sexual restrictions associated to copulation during breastfeeding.

- Polygyny guaranteed that women of marriageable age were bestowed off because the ratio of women to men were greater and naturally as well as during war, men tend to die in greater numbers. Also, genetically women are tougher than men and men often showcase their masculinity by engaging in harmful brawls.

- In most of cultural Africa, there was a tradition of widow inheritance i.e. when a man dies, his male siblings inherits the wife, and this was so in order to provide support for the children of the widow and to bear more children.

- Children and women were better secured against aggressors. Pride was linked with a larger family but low self-esteem and shame was related with small families, which symbolizes poverty.

- Diversity in sexual partners and sexual gratification is one of the reasons why men embrace polygyny. However, in some communities it is forbidden to copulate during women's pregnancy and menstruation, therefore polygyny proffers a solution to this issue.

Polygyny contributes to the low saving rate in Africa because even if the human capital i.e. labour produces effective food production for consumption and for commercial purposes, the cost of taking care of the family solely depends on the patriarchy and the amount available to support the family.

CHAPTER 5

ROLE OF POLYGYNY IN FAMILY MISTRUST ISSUES.

Family is one of the important social inclusions and relation a person develops, it is the first form of socialization to which a child develops how to communicate and interact with its immediate society and recognize each other and others. Polygyny has been established as a family structure or a marital state where one husband is married and sexually involved with more than one woman at the same time which has a notable effect on the academic achievements, social adjustment, education, mental health of kids from a polygamous family. The competing interest of wives for husband's attention is known as the pervasive alliance and cooperation as well as coexistence of extensive conflicts in family arrangements.

Co-operative conflict model is an excellent representation of polygyny in Sub-Saharan Africa, as it plays a key role in organizing wives' access to provisions important for their health and that of their offspring. Polygyny is a common and accepted form of marital system in many African countries today, there have been cases where a man marries two wives on the same day in this 21st century in western parts of Africa. Polygyny organizes social relation within the family by demanding collaboration among coexisting wives in effective productivity (agricultural and domestic), as well as reproductive (conjugal and child conception) grounds, while being under the husband's authority to whose parental assets and utmost attention are in straight competition. According to history, polygyny is related to agrarian, patrilineal, gerontocracy societies that restrict women's access to inheritance, and support from biological relations and foundation of dignified powers.

Polygyny is a practice common in Africa, as it is where it popularly exist right before the emerging of Christianity and Islam in Africa. For paternal lineages, polygyny is considered as wealth in people as it's not only multiplying offspring but promotes political association via in-laws as well as the increase of field productivity. Considering the views of power balance, wives are under authority of the husband and his ancestry line especially the mother of the husband, for right to essential resources and support during child conception as well as other events of life. The ability of wives to negotiate this social relationships to their favour and that of their child within context and that of their fellow wives is crucial to their satisfaction as well as that of their children. Chronologically, first wives are treated with respect and are regarded as the family 'manager', and a measure of liberation from husband who shows special attention to younger co-wives.

Competition among co-wives is increased if women directly depend on the husband for access to resources as well as emotional fulfilment, thereby causing breeding ground for household mishaps and conflict amidst wives and children and causing mistrust amongst mothers and their children with fellow wives. Rivalry amongst wives is fiercest around the investment of the husband on the health, education and general wellbeing of the children especially male child whose conception guarantees the bond of husband to wife and who will cater for them in their old age. In spite of a dignified egalitarian rotation of domestic and marital duties, sexual and emotional favouritism is show by the husband. Strategies like the 'divide and conquer' prevent wives from blending in cooperative passive resistance. The outcome is sometimes often imposed socially to result into prisoner's quandary, to which co-existing wives must select either unifying with one another or contending for the influence in their personal relationships with their husband. Rivalry between co-wives is heightened in the migratory setting, as wives compete to make the most of their reproductive value and to manipulate their status in nations where just one wife can get health benefits of process identity documents. Equally, co-operation of co-wives can result into economies of scale, which may permit women to go after remunerative activities outside the family, catering for themselves and children during times of insecurity.

Polygyny and How It Contributes To the Health Vulnerabilities of Women.

Susceptibility to STIs is perhaps the most widely identified health consequences of polygyny, the advent of terms such as sidagamie in West Africa, mpendo wa kando and dhoom tok in East Africa or side-chick is the outcome and effect of the transmission of STIs and HIV. Demographic variables partially described the effect of polygyny on the transmission of STI. Mental health, fertility, exposure factors, and susceptibility to sexually transmitted disease or infections are below discussed:

1. **Mental health:** Unlike reproductive health, mental health of women in polygyny settings. Women in polygamous homes

experience more dissatisfaction than women living in a nuclear family. Jealousy and anxiety can be worsened by aggression between co-wives; there have been accusations and allegations to poisoning and witchcraft thereby causing mistrust within the household. Polygyny also contributes to increase rate of physical, emotional and sexual abuse.

2. **Exposure factors**: the percentage of single women in polygyny with the social order is low. Though, polygyny causes marital uncertainty, divorce presents little possibilities to women's fertility as they remarry fast or engaged in private sexual satisfaction.

3. **Vulnerability to sexually transmitted diseases or infections:** Polygyny modifies a husband's sexual and emotional relationship to his spouses in order to increase the risk of transmission of STI. Lack of communication about sexual health status with spouses and emotional loose ties contributes to the transmission of STDs and STIs as well as vital treatments to be taken. Even though wives request the use of condom or other protective forms of sexual intercourse, the husband may assume infidelity issues to the wife. Polygyny can contribute to marital uncertainty with

concurrent rates of divorce, family disintegrations occur, socially dysfunctional emerge, socioeconomic disadvantaging becomes norms and continuation of intergeneration of disadvantage children arise as a medium of future. Ensuring utmost fidelity to their husbands, wives are dissatisfied sexually, emotionally and materially thereby making them prone to have more than one sexual partner outside relationship.

Household mistrust is very rampant in large families and prone to aggression where everything seems to be competitive including space and child bearing. This contributes to several health burdens, socioeconomics and social repercussions that also influenced the poverty rate in African families. Therefore, it is imperative to educate and also advice based on ignorance or personal decisions that having more than one wife or many unmanageable children contributes to socioeconomic disadvantaged children, emotional disorientation, physical abuse, socially imbalance and material contribution making the home extremely volatile.

The mistrust between the husband and his wives generated unwavering hatred within the polygyny unit, where children become as victims and disadvantage one.

CHAPTER 6

ROLE OF POLYGYNY IN THE ADOLESCENT STAGE OF AN AFRICAN CHILD.

The adolescent stage of any child's life is very critical as it shapes the perspective of life of such child. Growing up with constant competing for space, food, necessary resources, father's affection, snuggling and attention are always a challenges to children in large monogyny and polygyny families. Children from large monogamous and polygamous families are dissatisfied and prone to aggression behaviours resulting in low self-esteem and low academic performance. Although, there is apparent evidence of easy social inclusion and relation but inherent hate and rivalry is sometimes prevalent especially when theirs is obvious case of rivalry and chaos in family relationships. To the society, this pose a large threat to the interaction and evidence of jealousy is obvious when it comes to cooperate ownership of a certain asset.

Polygyny also contributes to strife and jealousy within the family especially when the paternal head of house is deceased and the sharing of inheritance is concerned. Asides having a dominated negative emotion against steps families, ambivalence, apathy and negative reactions are evidential in the attitudes of step teenagers when interacting with stepmother or stepsiblings. The relation is better comprehended with dislike, jealousy, disownment, hatred, condemnation and blame. Unfortunately, these emotions are not only apparent in family and sibling relationship; there is transmission of mistrust and resentment passed down to relationships with spouses or partners. With the partial withdrawal of father's attention and financial support, there are cases where the bond of siblings gets stronger especially children of the same mother, experiences shared outlines how the polygamous nature of their father influenced a larger extent of affectionate, supporting, reliance financial and emotional dependence amongst siblings.

The practice of polygyny was outlined with several negative experiences like the breakdown of the family, educational limitations, sense of deficit, social dysfunction and economic constraints. According to the research carried out by Aneeza Pervez & Syeda Shahida Batool (2016) participants of the research shared the formation of strained, distant and impaired by their father's second or third marriage which is then written off by conflict, lack of trust, and condemnation. Children from polygamous homes considered their father inaccessible, manipulative, selfish and materialistic.

At adolescent stages, children needs the attention and affection of a father figure in their lives to advise them as well as guard them through the troubling and perplexing forms of life, if absent due to polygamous reasons, children resent their father as they view it as their father being selfish as he only gave preferential treatment to his new bride. There is no father-to-child trust in existence in polygamous homes, as the presence of a new bride as crushed the trust the children have on him. According to Shepard 2013, the position of the mother of the child inside the family as well as family size is a vital factor disturbing women in polygamous relationship. Individuals who are living or have lived in a polygamous home will face poor interpersonal relationship challenges, which affect the success and continuous functioning of individual in different spheres of life. There is a possibility of long-term instabilities in the future romantic and marital relationships of adolescents in the society.

Fundamental relationship and involvement of father in the life of an adolescent child is crucial in the development of the child. Also, social and emotional development of an adolescent is dependent on the family forms and social interaction within the family unit. Therefore, the role of the father in keeping a polygamous home harmonized is very crucial in order to curb breeding grounds for children mental health instabilities, social menace problems, academic difficulties etc. Also, there are cases of diverse similarities discovered including depression, self-esteem, hostility, anxiety, learning disorders as well as other psychological and emotional disorders associated with attitudinal and behavioural problems. Comparing monogamous family with polygamous families, in children there are often few cases related to learning and attitudinal problems in large monogamous families but not as compared to polygamous families (Aneeza Pervez & Syeda Shahida Batool, 2016).

Rivalry amongst co-wives frequently prove damaging to children in polygamous families, also the thoughts and beliefs which the children are faced with are controlled permitting the indirect learning of polygamist beliefs, in the words of (Ward, 2004) it blinds the children from the world outside polygyny. The thoughts and beliefs about marriage is that polygyny is the perfect form of marriage; hence the male child takes after the polygamous nature of his father. Offspring in polygamous marriages are prone to experience psychological distress, low self-esteem, marital discord, and face abuse. Concurrent marital fights and distress can result into emotional and psychological harm to children and they undergo unequal preferential treatment, tension, conflict, jealousy from the father, (Elbedour et al., 2002).

Teenagers from polygamous home feel discontented and disconnected from their families, particularly from their father as no emotional support whatsoever is received due to the large number of other siblings. With no definite family structure, adolescents of polygamous home are most times confused as to the accepted family structure. Unfortunately, children of polygamous homes are prone to conflict and stress, also increased degree of violence and fights between parents (Elbedour et al., 2012). There is a damning issue of the child having difficulty in developing confidence, sense of trust, security and self-esteem. Influenced by the stress and challenges faced by their mothers, adolescent children experience the closeness and affection of their mothers more than their father. As the family tends to become larger, the more the stressful modifications imposed on children.

Studies has also showed that adolescent children of polygamous home have lesser chances of interacting with their parents particularly their father and may not enjoy the reception of parental support. As expected, these kids may also experience rivalry, envy and jealousy from their half siblings. According to the research conducted by Elbedour, Bart, and Hektner (2010) depicts that kids from larger polygamous families have faintly reduced level of unity than children of nuclear families, hence there is a likelihood of display of socialization issues and also psychopathological warning sign.

CHAPTER 7

CONSEQUENCES OF FINANCIAL DISHONESTY IN COUPLES.

Quality communication is arguably the best panacea to any and every marital troubles. This chapter elucidates the cause and effect of financial dishonesty amongst couples and how it can be averted. In ancient times, the man is regarded as the sole breadwinner of the family, this results to lots of pressure enacted on the man to support and cater for his family as well as extended family particularly in Africa. Dishonesty and insincerity in couples is very dangerous and lays the foundation of destroying the marriage, it also influence the advent of polygyny. Financial fidelity is the bedrock of a successful home. Being honest about financial transactions and capacity is as significant as being faithful in a marriage. Although in today's world, several couples have the strong tendency of seeing one another naked than sharing the details of their account statements. Wealth is one of the key causes of frustration and hassles in marriages and family relationships. There is a direct important relationship between finance and happy homes or successful romantic relationships.

Financial dishonesty is synonymous to cheating; it can quickly frustrate a once happy relationship. Financial dishonesty is any cash-related mien that involves one partner being less faithful or unaccountable with money than the other romantically involved partner or spouse. At first it begins with inconsequential amounts and then graduates into blowing up the savings on an illogical wants such as pair of shoes or piece of jewellery. With time, the financial white lies get more dawning and the untruthful spouse may defend his or her spending actions by vindicating that it is vital for future financial security. Financial dishonesty individuals habitually cover up any illogical money attitudes that they suppose their spouse may frown on and hide their dishonest money attitude on how the other faithful partner uses their cash.

A classic example involves the saving and spending spouse who attempt to settle both their financial perspective and incompatibilities like balancing a transaction. Financial dishonesty is also when the saving spouse carts away into savings some money for rainy days against the knowledge of the other spouse. There should be communication and consensual agreement between both parts on how much to save and how much to be spent, when either of this is done with prior knowledge of one party, then it is referred to as financial dishonesty. Some common warning signs of probable financial dishonesty in couples includes:

- When one's spouse is less forthcoming about their finances,

- When one's partner insists on having a separate account and possess secretive code words for their banking platforms,

- Suspicious withdrawals from joint accounts,

- When one's partner only wants to control the money with no basic money input,

- When one's partner changes the subject anytime money talks comes up.

Here are some useful hints on how to improve money communications between couples.

1. Reduce or remove individual accounts and agree to make them joints where transaction statements will be shared by both spouse.

2. Both couples should be included in the paying of bills as it helps create and balance of credits and debits.

3. Be outright honest with your spouse about asset and monetary declarations. Settle any disputes regarding money quite early to avoid getting more complicated.

Mending financial dishonesty can be hard, if not possible, several couples that have experienced it, finds it difficult to overcome. Nonetheless, getting advice and consultations from trained experts or people who have gone through this may help proffer solution to resolve the money dispute and attend to the source it originates from. This should be done imperatively before legal actions and proceedings is the sole attention of the affronted party.

Below are few useful tips for arbitrating financial infidelity in one's marital relationship:

1. Recognize and acknowledge your financial personality,

2. Look for safe forums for both you and your spouse to discuss the reasons behind your monetary behaviours as well as the driving force behind your spending or saving conduct,

3. Formulate a forward moving and all-inclusive consensus to avoid future misunderstandings over money, and

4. Assert on and devise a plan to influence and guarantee full

financial limpidity in order to rebuild honesty between spouses.

Influence the mutual knowledge and experience of financial planners and experts, mediators, therapists, marriage consultants and any other professionals and how much positive influence on the role money plays in your marital relationship.

The cost of deception in one's finances either on a small or large scale can be grossly damaging to one's financial and romantic relationship. Some consequences of financial dishonesty includes, lack of trust, divorce, arguments, separation, division of finances etc. While in some cases, some couples see the need to salvage the situation and proffer logical panacea, and it has helped them grow much closer as a couple and there is much cooperation and involvement than before. Also, budgeting of allowance and money plans are also helpful steps to help rejuvenate trust and togetherness in the marriage. Money talks should be scheduled more often, and a time of the month of the week should be scheduled so as to avoid abrupt money discussions with lack of interest of the other party. Hiding debts and investments have great consequences as it shows the spouse lies, to which it is a form of cheating i.e. cheating on your partner's knowledge.

Enough time should be set aside to settle such infidelity acts.

Hoarding financial information from one's spouse may not last a long time, as the truth will eventually find its way out. Couples disagree most times about how money should be handled as well as lack the management and prudent skill to reach logical solutions to attain financial freedom.

Below are some tips by Dr Bonnie on how to bring on financial freedom and put an end to financial infidelity.

- Classify financial issues from other issues,

- Be sensitive to your spouse's timing,

- Create separate account for bills, savings, investment and luxuries,

- When having money discussions, be open and honest with your partner and do not be judgmental.

- Deliberate expenditures of large amount with your spouse.

- Reward yourself with incentives for money talks.

However, money should not be a deal breaker with your spouse and carefully revisit financial expectations per week.

CHAPTER 8

GENDER EQUALITY AMONGST CHILDREN

In Africa, the girl child is considered inferior to the male child, several tribes in most developing rural part of Africa believes the place of a female child is to domestic and reproductive purposes. Inequality has led to diverse degree of unfairness in terms of education and human rights to the girl child. Worse off is when a girl is betrothed to a man before she reaches puberty and escorted to her betrothed spouse in order to form alliances or seal business or political deals. Faced with diverse illogical discrimination in the family unit, the girl child is deprived of essential educational rights. The contribution of the female child in agriculture has help boost the productivity of a community; naturally the female gender is characterized with multitasking and hard work. Therefore, this has led to the recognition by most African governments that encouraging women can help to alleviate poverty in larger families. Education and formal literacy is a major contributor to economic development.

Also, it has come into the knowledge of African governments that the transition in the fertility of Africa i.e. a crucial factor in continuous economic growth, which appears to be at a slower pace than the rest of the world. Poverty, poor access to quality schooling, lack of quality social norms and sanitary facilities. This makes demeaning acts prevalent in Eastern African countries, \and Southern Africa countries i.e. such as female genital mutilation, early child marriage a norm and hinders the female child from knowing her fundamental right. Therefore school enrolment for the female child into primary, secondary and tertiary formal educational institution is lower in terms of rate of boys enrolment in countries such as Eritrea, South Sudan, Mozambique, Angola and much lower in the continent as a whole.

Poverty in larger African families can be drastically reduced when the female child is enrolled into an educational institution, gaining formal knowledge and experience improves the dissemination of vital information regarding female basic rights, access to maternal health services as well as family planning initiatives, this will reduce the rate of fertility and rapid population growth as well as improve economic prospect for women. Innovative ways are being sought by some governments in Africa on how to quicken the demographic evolution. It is most times argued that the ticket out of poverty is education, particularly education for the girl child. Inequalities between boys and girls start from the basic primary school and the disparities increase through the full educational system. In total admission into primary education, Africa recorded the highest comparative increase among regions during the last ten years, however given the low proportion of girls registered into schools, Africa is still far behind from accomplishing intake of equality. Sub-Saharan Africa was noted as the only region with high percentage of girls out of school in the year 2000.

This is the time where gender equality should favour the girl child as it has been proven over and over again that the education of a child is one great strategy that is cost-effective which helps promote economic growth and development of the society. Evidently speaking, research has shown that a female right to education has practically improved the rate of development to their families and personal accomplishment. Literate women tend to have well-nourished and healthier babies, and strive to ensure their children both gender are educated in reducing the damning cycle of poverty in the society. Gender equality sensitization should be stressed particularly in the Sub-Saharan parts of Africa, due to the inferiority and weak stamina characterized with feminism several opportunities are taken away from the girl child and ignorantly bypassed.

In addition, rigorous sensitization and dissemination of information should be done in the rural areas that no gender is superior to the other, also it is not forbidden or a taboo for a girl to participate and put into action her human rights independently. Patriarchy in Africa is a strong force to reckon with especially in the rural areas of developing countries in Africa, many perceptions as to opportunities are believed to be best handled by only the male figure in the family. Polygyny may come about when a man has been conceiving the female child in search of a male offspring, and keeps trying until a male is conceived and then regarded as the successor of the head of the household.

Gender inequality and stereotyping against the girl child can be reduced significantly to elimination when government of different regions commence initiatives that introduce gender-sensitive curriculum and encourage the enrolment of the female gender into schools. Careful and well explicit programs should be conducted in rural areas to sensitive and influence the prospects of gender equality, career choices for girls without discrimination, and how the female gender play a vital role in the progress of the country and continent as a whole. Full participation and completion of enrolment the girl child will influence the decision to participate in the political, social and economic development of Africa. Realizing the power of the female gender at a tender age will help the female child develop self-esteem and help harness the full her full potentials.

Several demeaning acts to feminism like rape, abuse, violation of girl rights, violence against women emotionally and physically will be fought against and held with utmost contempt thereby reducing the rate of mortality of female child at attender age. Gender equality will bring into halt the perspective of confusion in identity where females (girl or woman) will not be referred to as a possession to be owned but as a human being. Elimination of gender stereotyping will influence the freedom of identity of the female and allow them not live under the influence of patriarchy authorities only. Gender equality is a breath of fresh air to females all over the world as it screams liberation from all forms of cultural shackles.

CHAPTER 9

GENDER EXPECTATION AND EARLY MARRIAGE OF THE GIRL CHILD.

The amount of expectation and pressure placed on the girl child at a very tender age in most developing countries is alarming. Aside being stripped of carrying the family legacy due to gender, they are being married off to either form alliances or affiliation politically or economically. The girl child carries so much domestic and reproductive responsibilities on how to cater for her household and spouse only as her main focus in life, this result into pervasive rate of early child marriage as well as less than normal access to quality education and quality lifestyle as a human being ultimately. The devastating consequence of early marriage is the fact that a much tender age even as children, girls are expected to prove their fertility thereby making them mothers even as children.

Marriage and how to take care of family unit becomes the only life known and aspired for by the child bride, with little or no strong wage employment potentials, the female child bride depends majorly on her husband for provision. This exposes her to the risk of abusive relationship, which only lives with no options than to leave with children and also increases the rate of abject poverty in the continent. Initiatives such as 'Girls not Bride' was established as an association of civil society agencies due to shared belief on the important role of rural activism, in due course, change will occur in the lives of female especially girls and their immediate environment when family unit and communities put an end to child marriage and accept the roles for girls beyond shared marital vows.

Based on the convention of Human Rights council held in Geneva, it was established that for girls, discrimination and stereotyping on the grounds of gender and sex begins from birth. Also, countries with law structures and policies that comply with the agreements and because of cultural customs, tradition as well as the letdown to implementing domestic legal provisions and often times at childhood girls end up being victims of discrimination. Forced early girl child marriage is the thief of most girls' childhood, confidence and self-esteems; it hinders girls from active involvement in the world outside their community as well as the exploration and finding of their true self and potential. Unknowingly to them they are experiencing abusive and violating relationships but thinks it is being submissive.

The complete controls over reproductive and sexual rights of young females as well as lack of bodily autonomy are the main cause of forced girl child early marriage. Early marriage of the girl child and forced marital commitment results to greater chances of violation of reproductive and sexual rights of younger females noting that they are more than likely to be faced with sexual violence. Inflexible and choking control over girl's and women's human and civil rights in order to guard their chastity and upgrade family honour, it makes sure that female child have no other choice to explore their sexuality but only within their marriage. In most developing countries, the contexts and stigma over deflowering a female before marriage is very high leading to elevated risk of violence within the family and in the community.

In larger African homes, gender based chores or labour happens when certain roles assigned to a particular gender, thereby the perspective of women being suitable as domestic workers has affected girls in terms of gender expectation. In Kenya for example, most girls are experiencing distress as regards the effects of child domestic chores. Girls are often depended on to work in municipal households and also in South Sudan, girl child labour is worst to the core as it comes with abusive obligations, discriminations and heavily denied access to basic human rights. Domestic child labourers are compelled by the plight of poverty mostly at a very young age. Early marriage is therefore is form of sexual and physical abuse on a young girl child who suffered the emotional and physical pain that goes with the practice of early marriage. Sufficient funds should be set aside for the sensitizing of rural communities, local administrators and schools teachers to report any incidence to authorities for prompt action. Rescue centres that are reliable should be set up to the girl child that absconded or rescued from early marriages practice as well as abuse experienced due to child labour. The security operatives should be involved about sexual abuses and violations, perpetrators and accused persons should be apprehended and prosecuted accordingly.

Child prostitution in Africa should be handled with strict measures of prosecution and punishments as this not only violate the girl child emotionally, physically, sexually but also socially and health wise. It exposes them to the vulnerability of being susceptible to diseases and worse HIV/AIDS. Paedophilic acts on the girl child should be duly punished and lockout for life. Correctional and rehabilitation centres should be established for easy counselling and recuperating from the traumas and abuse experienced. Also, African governments should go extra by providing resources to support the families of the girl child as the plight of poverty in the family prompted the early marriage, child labour, abuse and prostitution in the first place. Complete development will not be achieved if gender, the girl child continues to be marginalized and prone to marital, sexual and physical abuse and violation.

The role of the male child in putting an end to early child marriage and gender expectation of the girl child is crucial. As the saying 'charity begins at home' goes so does the elimination of gender expectation can be reduced, for instance when domestic chores are being piled up boys can also be shared the same portion of work to ensure fairness. In as much as poverty in larger family is concerned, with the advent of gender equality acceptance and application in most parts of developing countries in Africa, labour and chores should be shared according to one's capacity and effectiveness and not just due to gender status. Also, when the male gender (boy, father, brother, etc.) is allies in the wiping out of gender expectation and early child marriage helps structure a promising prospect for the female gender in the future.

CHAPTER 10

THE CONCEPT OF DOWRY IN AFRICAN HOMES.

Dowry is an important of African culture as it is one of the prerequisite rites to be done before marriage. As rich as Africa is with tribes and culture, the dowry rites of different tribes differs and are interesting concepts. In this chapter, the concept of dowry will be explicitly explained for easy understanding. Many westerners often mistake this rites as selling off the bride to the groom's household, however it has inherent cultural meaning and should not be mistaken for selling off the bride. All around Africa, the ancient custom of dowry remains a major pillar to the joining of man and wife in matrimony.

For instance, the Zulu tribe of South Africa dowry process is referred to as Lobola, the Yoruba tribe of West Africa refers to it as Idana, also in East Africa, Tanzania precisely called it Mahari and in Dinka tribe in South Sudan dowry process is referred as Thiik. In larger parts of the Sub-Saharan Africa, history reveals that dowry practice or bride price was borne from a cattle-based and agricultural based economy where riches and status were shown by how large one's family is and how much livestock is in one's possession. A wedding signifies the loss of a daughter in the household, hence the loss of additional labour and a feminine figure that takes care of the younger ones in the family. Therefore, the groom gifting the bride's household by paying dowry or bride price of gifts of livestock and farm produce to replenish the loss of labour and also act as a source of food i.e. goats and cows are gifted to the bride's household as gifts. However, in the modern era, there have been modifications in the gift items, most times money is used in place of livestock gifts and agricultural produce.

Dowry and bride price are often mistaken for acts of misogyny, however, the family system of most African countries are patrilineal and patriarchal. To ensure continuity of custom and clan, marriage is inevitable. Dowry payment nowadays in usually in form of money but in the ancient times it is done in forms of exchange of different kinds of livestock especially goats or cows which may be done in a few days before the wedding ceremony or on a long-term basis based on agreement between the two households, which is mostly from the time of conception to years after marriage. Dowry is an evidence of legality and justice to both families involved, with the unfortunate rise in the trend of divorce, the custom of dowry payment is considered as a variable that links the community to the durable moral standards of ancient times because the woman feels worthy to her husband and may remain faithful to the marriage vows shared.

On the contrary, in Kenya for instance, educated, urban-centric individuals are of the opinion that marriage is based on love, understanding and not like the olden days where one is betrothed at a young age and expects love to come around in the journey of the marriage. They argue against dowry as being misogynistic as it builds the marriage on fear and on economic and financial variables and the only motivation to faithfulness in the marriage is the fear of the bride's parent returning the dowry to the groom's family should in case the marriage ends up a fiasco. Comparatively, South Sudan as the least developed African country remained as a traditional state and most patriarchal society in Africa if not entire world; it's a country where traditional marriages are huge source of wealth. Most young girls marriages among Dinka tribe accounted between 30 - 200 herds of cattle. In western countries like Australia, Canada and United States of America where majority of Dinka people of South Sudan resided, traditional marriages are skyrocketing accounting between $30,000 to $80,000 dowry payments to bride's parent, this is excluding preparation of wedding and new home establishment for newly marriage couple. Consequently, this greediness has brought about discouragement to young people growing up in western world and again it does leave newly wed couple economically disadvantaged. In addition, it is argued that the wife is seen in a demeaning perspective where she is subjected to being referred to as a commodity that can be exchanged with money. In large poor households in Sub-Saharan Africa, if not based on love, the wife is enslaved in the marriage thereby being at high risk of violence and abuse from her spouse.

With the increased rate of poverty in Africa, in larger households the female children are at a disadvantage stages because the poor parents think of the dowry as a ticket to take them out from poverty. When it comes to inheritance, the men are favoured to control labour, income and property. Therefore, it is against this milieu that the custom of dowry for the joining in matrimony is bit by bit eroding. Away from the urban-centric views of dowry, although there is no fixated cost for dowry in terms of money neither is there a fixed number of goats and cattle to be brought. However, when a girl is educated, it is established that the cost of her dowry is increased, hence, woman is an asset traditionally and if educated is worthy of a reasonably attractive dowry.

In recent times, it has been noted that greed has made dowry expensive, in East and West Africa particularly the Dinka and the Igbo tribes respectively, it has been discovered that exorbitant dowry and traditional rites are being asked for from the groom's household. Although, it is not permitted to say in front of one's in-law that they are greedy but most times they are avaricious. On the list may include goats, cows, huge sum of money sometimes in foreign currency, a house or a cow but do not often follow through on the requirements. Most times, the concern is the financial aspect of the dowry i.e. money that is of utmost importance. Customarily, dowry is simply a token of affection and gratitude to the parent and household of the bride but due to the poverty level of Africa and covetousness of the bride's household, it has led to a typical business transaction. Dowry in the olden times connotes the determination and seriousness of the groom to the bride but nowadays it is linked to fees that do not warrant assurance and sustainability in couple relationships. This sudden change of dowry from affection and appreciation to fees and forms of business has degraded the essence of dowry in culture and reduced into to the demeaning act of transaction of commodity. Alternatively, the groom can offer several forms of assistance to the bride's household at a reasonable pace and not be put under pressure or be forced to carry out philanthropic duties alone instead of in-law to relative duties.

CHAPTER 11

THE MISCONCEPTIONS OF WIFE OWNERSHIP IN AFRICA.

Detailed explicitly in the previous chapter, marriage at an early age and due to poverty to form alliance or be a ticket out of hunger for the household leaves the bride enslaved to which she endures and not to enjoy her marital union. Majorly, dowry has always been viewed from the male's perspective, although marriage is found to be complex across all tribes. The major misconceptions mostly among African men have concerning dowry payment is that they 'own' the bride, either betrothed to them at a very tender age or married off to the groom at the first stage of puberty. With the demeaning perspective that the bride is a possession to own, many wives are seen as slaves to their husband and only abide by the judgments and commandments of their spouse to the extent they depend on him both financially and emotionally.

The traditional impact that wife ownership has on women is also an influencing variable that contributes to the spread of HV/AIDS. In a Washington Post written by Mark Mathabane, he shared how his South African sister was affected negatively with the issue of bride price and wife ownership. The article centred on the practice of dowry, which is referred to as lobola in which the customary rites of dowry are performed by the exchange of money or livestock with the bride. Mark also stated that the practice is one of the reasons why women are more affected by the spread of HIV/AIDS than men in Southern Africa region. Due to the affordability of the dowry, it promotes polygyny and the creation of large families. Dowry, paedophilic acts, rape, and other forms of sexual abuse on girls experiencing early marriages are one of the main reasons for the rapid spread of HIV/AIDS amongst young females.

Large family acknowledge and influences infidelity, thereby putting other wives at potential risk of infection with sexually transmitted diseases or infections and worse HIV/AIDS. Most wives endure their marriages by staying through the hardship and pain, because of the societal myth that a woman who is not a widow should stay back in her marriage till she can submit completely to her husband wishes. Female oppression as also going back may bring reproach to her family, hence the continuous abuse and unhappiness lingers. Setting up of campaigns that are for preventive measures, education and drug research by most African governments will be effective if the discrimination and stereotyping is addressed enthusiastically. Dowry has been addressed as a defensive mechanism that serve as a measure to stabilize the marriage, protect her against several forms of abuse from her husband, and joining of two separate families, however, this defence mechanism do not withstand great pressure under examination.

With the commercialization of dowry and bride price, a combination of cash and livestock is mostly given to the bride household in recent times. The outcome of the payment of dowry is now used as a means of meeting daily expenses in poor large household rather than being used to keep financial security for widowed or divorced wife. Additionally, the ridiculous hike in the demands of dowry and bride price has rendered it difficult for most young men who cannot afford it to enter into informal union which results into the undermining of the marriage institution and what it stands for and further condemns many children into being conceived out of wedlock. Also, the union of the two families due to marriage has drifted away from its initial purposes; dowry is not viewed as a payment to the father of the bride alone and not to the relations.

Biased wife ownership practiced in Africa has rendered the payment of dowry useless in the sense that once the exorbitant price of dowry rites have been given and performed, the husband views the wife as a most priced commodity and can do whatsoever tickles his fancy to the wife. Modern developments have made dowry outlived its worth as property rights, domestic violence, polygyny, patriarchy, and wife inheritance are distinct features that results to the dowry usefulness being outlived. Also, biased wife ownership is used as a selfish tool to fulfil the personal needs of husbands as well as used to control their wives to their economic, social, sexual and emotional detriment. The vast diminished power of women in sexual negotiations, economic and political agreements, it also influences the rapid spread of human deadly disease such as Blood Born Viruses, HIV and AIDS. Women worldwide are more than half of the people living with HIV/AIDS according to UNAIDS.

Besides, dowry and its role in the spread of HIV/AIDS is that, during African traditional union, when the dory is paid the woman is stripped off the right to own properties, therefore any property she might have own prior to her marriage now belongs to her husband. Abusive and violations in marriages are endured by the wife in order not to be sent away empty handed, because since all properties owned by her has been customarily given to the husband, therefore the rate of being infected with STDs or STIs is heightened. Wife ownership especially in early marriages depicts an increase in forced sexual violations, rape, battered and gender violence. In addition, sociocultural practices such as female genital mutilation, early marriages, wife sexual sharing and widow inheritance continues as a result of biased wife ownership.

Wife ownership (biased) has contributed into increased risk of poverty; the stripping off inheritance from the wife and widow sharing when the husband is deceased contributes to human rights violation as well as sexual violation of the widow. Without prior interest, the woman is being passed down like a piece of used property to be maintained by the deceased brother, worst is if the woman has children, she is expected to bear more children for the 'new' husband thereby contributing to polygamy and increased rate of population. Activism and campaigns should be done in order to sensitize and educate women about their rights as well as their worth.

CHAPTER 12

CONCEPT AND MISCONCEPTION OF FAMILY PLANNING IN AFRICA.

The issue of increase in population is undeniably the outcome of the unmet need for family planning. The rate of married women who are prolific and sexually active but are willing to delay or put a stop to child conception but lack the knowledge or have misconceptions about family planning is high especially in the rural Sub-Saharan parts of Africa. Practice and application of services of family planning in developing countries of Africa have been discovered to prevent unintended prenatal period, reduce child and maternal death; however, the practice is recorded to be very low. Family planning services is widely recognized as an essential intervention towards accomplishing Millennium Development Goals 4 & 5 as it has been verified to lower mortality of mother and child. Unsafe abortions and unwanted prenatal periods can be prevented with family planning.

Affordable family planning methods that can be readily available to people living in rural areas is the use of condom which can protect unwanted pregnancies, and also protects individuals from STDs and STIs as well as HIV-AIDS. Lack of adequate knowledge about the socioeconomic benefits of family planning with unmet need for child spacing has led to the continuous cycle of larger families in Africa. However, when information on what family planning is, method appropriate and available, as well as information on how to obtain to them is being disseminated to them, it will improve child spacing and reduce maternal and infant mortality. In addition, family planning has been found to influence economic and educational empowerment of the female gender and also influence gender equality. Regardless of the perks, the acceptance and uptake of family planning in Sub-Saharan Africa is still meagre.

Low uptake of family planning has led to heightened rate of unwanted pregnancies, unsafe abortions, unplanned deliveries, maternal, and infant mortalities in most developing countries of Africa. This can be blamed on several variables, observations have led to the conclusion that sensitization and alertness of the availability and benefits of family planning will improve its responsiveness and uptake. Asides the awareness and uptake of family planning, participants should be duly and appropriately counselled on the various types of family planning and the type that works best as well as how it works. Women should be properly advised and counselled on the side effects of some types of family planning so as to avoid abrupt halt of the use of contraceptives. Another hindrance to the uptake of family planning is the distance and difficulty in accessing quality family planning services as they are provided in health facilities far away from their residence. Moreover, religious beliefs and inclination has been a major force against family planning in Africa, although some individuals believe family planning is basically for the use of married couples however, some fear that the initiative may be abused and result into sexual promiscuity.

Misconceptions and Myths of Family Planning.

Majorly, religious and cultural beliefs are particularly the main constraints of the usage of forms of family planning. The women believes their spouse, family, religion, community is opposed to contraception. An additional limitation to the use of family planning forms is the misconception and myths about urban methods, like erroneous or overstated reports about side effects, negative stereotypes about individuals who practice family planning and misconceptions about the short or long-term health issues. For instance, in developing and developed countries, several women erroneously think the use of oral contraceptives to be more harmful than prenatal periods. Misconceptions like this can rapidly spread as rumours via informal communications by words of mouth or other social and informal channel of information dissemination, which continually results into negative opinions. The occurrence of these misconceptions has been severally demonstrated in rural areas to national level.

Low demand of the use of family planning methods is as a result of myths and misconceptions as well as incorrect and inadequate knowledge of contraceptives. Comprehending the collective impact of how misconceptions, beliefs and myth of family planning is associated with the uptake and use of contraceptive is key for the establishment of policies and programs that aim to influence contraceptive popularity. Suppressed demand for family planning may be explained into the actual use if programs can dismiss false perceptions about contraceptive usage. Besides, recognizing the misconception of family planning, which often reveals the attitudes and norms of the community, will show the importance of considering approaches that go beyond a person's level of knowledge and change in behaviour.

Educational programs are required to dismiss the misconceptions and myths of family planning. In Nigeria for instance, programs that promote community-based discussions may be active at lowering misconceptions and increasing modern use of contraceptive. In Talensi district, Ghana, it has been concluded that there is an imperative need for the office of directorate of health to strengthen health education on the perks of family planning with the male partner involved. African governments should intensify family planning services and make it more accessible thereby reduce the rate of larger families and rapid population growth in extreme poverty in Africa.

Some Typical Myths Associated with the Uptake of Family Planning.

1. In the countryside of Malawi, there is a popular belief among females that the use of contraceptive negatively affects the male sexual organs, resulting to the cause of impotence. Also, the use of condoms cause sores and blisters on the male genital organ while some perceive the use of condom have an oily substance which weakens sexual strength and kills the manhood.

2. The fear of weight loss to the extent people think they are

infected with HIV-AIDS, prolonged menstrual cycle makes the use of family planning methods slow.

3. In Nigeria, although very few Hausa women are aware of family planning, however they believe it is synonymous to murder in terms of moral. Their belief that children are a blessing and divine support and a remedy for mortality.

4. Customarily, having many children is seen as achievement of most families in South Sudan.

5. In Uganda, women believe the use of oral contraceptive is more harmful than prenatal periods, and also pills and injections can result into permanent infertility by harming the womb. Also, it is believed that pills can mount up into mass causing serious internal bleeding as well as mutation.

6. Contraceptive is associated with birth defects, infertility, growth of cancerous cells and loss of implant during sexual copulation leading to dire complications during birth.

All these myths further stresses the need to promote broad education of population mostly for females and also auspicious socioeconomic situations that constitute the important basics of use of family planning methods as well as subsequently manage the fertility and improved quality of life.

Sexual education and orientation is terribly low in Africa, most parents who are supposed to carry out this task on their young children consider it a taboo to discuss about sexual related topics with their children. This contributes to high degree of shared rumours as sex education is mostly taught by peers or worse experienced. Lack of knowledgeable sex education has resulted into grave consequences like untimely prenatal periods, widespread of the epidemic HIV-AIDS, the common practice of female genital mutilation, sexual abuse as well as increase in the mortality rate of mother and child. Oral contraceptives are active hormonal drugs that are taken by women on daily basis and may contain two hormones known as estrogen and progestagen. Birth control pills suppress the ovulation period but are slightly effective in more than half of women and the side effects includes coagulating of mucus discharged in the cervices hindering sperm penetration. A woman may ingest the oral pill if she is planning on getting sexually active or sexually active, oral contraceptives are 90-98% effective. Oral conception prevents pregnancy but produces shorter regular menstrual periods. It also protects women against infection of the fallopian tubes, ectopic pregnancies, ovarian and endometrial cancer.

Below are common misconceptions of birth control:

- Alterations in body weight: researches have proven that women on contraceptives do not gain more weight than those who are not.

- Contributes to general health issues: short-term side effects may be experienced as a result of usage which includes erratic change in menstrual periods, nausea, headaches, but they are not symptoms of illness and are sure to stop within few months of use. However, if symptoms persist, medical experts should prescribe another form of birth control. There are healthy perks to the use of birth control pills such as reduction in ovulation pain, reduction of menstrual cramps, protect against ovarian cancer, reduction in signs of polycystic syndrome etc.

- Loss of Libido: a number of women believe birth control contraceptive will reduce sexual desire and pleasure causing frigidity. The fact remains there is no proof, nor indication of how it affects sexual drive. Granting some women using this pill have testified that the pill either decreased or increased libido and performance, however, it is hard to determine whether it is as a result of the pill or life events.

- Pill Absorption: Several women are of the opinion that birth control pills amass in the body and cause tumours and disease or get stored in vital organs and form stones. The fact is after ingestion of the pill, it is broken down and dissolved into the digestive tracts and the hormones are absorbed into the bloodstream. When the contraceptive effect is produced, the hormones are used up in the gut and liver and are dispersed from the body and accumulated.

- Effective immediately after ingestion: this misconception is false, as in some women to prevented ovulation, a complete menstrual cycle is needed for the hormones to operate with the body's natural hormone. A 'plan B' method is often recommends by doctors on the first month of oral contraceptive use.

- Infertility or return to fertility: women who are concerned with family planning may wrongly believe that the use of oral birth control pills may result into long delay in conception and prevent future pregnancies. The point is that birth control pills does not cause infertility, it only prevent unwanted prenatal periods. There is therefore no proof that birth control delays a woman's fertility after days to months of non-use of oral birth control pills. Pregnancy for women who stops the use of contraceptives come as naturally and quickly just as non-participants. However, some non-birth control advantages of oral birth control pills include fertility preservation, protection against ectopic pregnancy, endometriosis and pelvic inflammatory diseases.

With these misconceptions debunked and facts coming into light, rural women can be educated and properly counselled to decide the form of birth control to use with the consent of her husband.

CHAPTER 13

CONCEPT AND MISCONCEPTION OF BIRTH CONTROL.

Birth control is simply one of the methods of family planning, medical experts counsels the female participants on the type of birth control contraceptive that best suits their plan. Research has shown that countries with the lowest rate of uptake of contraceptive suffers greatly from highest maternal, newborn, child mortality rates are in Africa. Just about 30% of all women who use birth control, though if it were accessible readily and available, more than half of African women will use birth control. The main issues that avert the access to and usage of birth control are poor healthcare facilities and services, religious and cultural beliefs, unavailability, deception about the side effects of birth control, spouse disapproval amongst many others. Condoms are the most accessible, available and affordable form of birth control. Quality of life of mother and child is improved, encourages economic development alongside decrease in maternal and newborn mortality when the use of birth control as well as other family planning method is increased.

Deleterious factors hindering or prohibiting the use of birth control is the misconceptions about the contraceptive, disapproval of the male partner, sociocultural norms girdling fertility. However, the positive factors include employment, education, communication and involvement of the male partner. Influencing the use of modern contraceptive in Africa specifically Sub-Saharan Africa is a multi-faceted issue that involves community, society and systems wide interventions that intends to counter negative misinformation and misconceptions. Public laws and policies as well as cultural behaviours play a role in the prevalence of birth control.

Myths and Misconceptions surrounding Birth Control.

Most studies carried out have concentrated on personal beliefs about contraception but myths are known to spread easily and faster with communities. It is therefore imperative to observe how the prevalence of deleterious myths in a community affects the cumulative level of method of use. Myths and misconceptions have been established as the major hindrance of the use of modern contraceptive. Asides, abstinence and menstrual periods that are natural ways of child spacing and controlling child conception, birth control is a much easier way to reduce the rapid growth of population and poverty in Africa. The influence of social network acceptance is stressed by several research conducted on the use of birth control beyond personal beliefs. Community meetings should be put in place to sensitize and teach women reasons why they should engage in family planning as well as the benefits and side effects that surrounds it. This can be done through large peer campaign approaches. In Kenya, population services created a mass media campaign to give lectures about major myths and misconceptions of birth control amongst youths.

To most rural parts of Sub Saharan developing countries of Africa, birth control is not a blessing. For instance, a terrorist group known as Boko Haram which terrifies north-eastern parts of Nigeria regards artificial contraception as a practice, product and act of infidel learning and therefore considered as taboo. Women are to avoid education and marry at an early age and bear lots of children. Polygyny is practiced at a large scale. Discussions of sexual matters amongst spouses is discouraged in other Sub-Saharan African traditions. Relatives and friends are used between partners for the exchange of opinions and ideas as well as problems pertaining to family planning and use of birth control contraceptives (DeRose et. al., 2004). To convey unequivocal sex-related information to each other, couples from these cultures may use any of the following forms of communication, i.e. wearing of particular waist beads, specific music, preparing of husband's favourite meals and acting a particular way (DeRose et. al., 2004). Pertaining to birth control, a man's contraceptive may in itself be a nonverbal display of consent. For that reason, discussions of this particular topic amongst couple will influence knowledge of birth control attitudes only when it augments the efficacy of or is more efficient than other forms of communication.

In Kenya, particularly cities of Bungoma and Nairobi, the major constraint to birth control includes lack of consent on the use of contraceptive use and on reproductive intents. Also, there are knowledge gaps on the forms of contraceptive, misconception about certain methods, fears from negative rumours, availability and poor quality of services, observed undesirable effects. Apparent disinterest in the continuation of children conception is recorded in approximately half of the wives in Bungoma and 33% in Nairobi (Rutenberg, N. and Watkins S.C., 1997). Lack of adequate communication and couples agreement are major reasons for non-use of birth control. Paralleled to South Sudan, patriarchy is with the authority and main decision maker. Due to apparent case of gender inequality, the husband desires to have more children if possible all male, as they are considered to have the capacity to provide financial security for their old parents.

Social stigma and deleterious stereotypes related with the use of contraception as well as sex limit uptake of contraception especially with youth. The custom norm of non-use of contraceptive is often deeply rooted and will require constant perseverance for gradual change to occur in spite of targeted intervention programs and campaigns. Early intervention is crucial especially when teenagers are forming their identities, and emerging their comprehension of social norms around gender and sexuality. Arrangements differs accordingly to urban or rural divides level of education. There is no certainty regarding the degree to which and in what way community-level social norms affects women and the use of modern contraceptives.

CHAPTER 14

DOMESTIC VIOLENCE AGAINST WOMEN AND CHILD (AFRICAN CONTEXT).

Domestic violence is a major crime against humanity and against the female gender in particular. In many parts of the world, married women are faced with different forms of domestic abuse, either physically, emotionally, financially and psychologically. The cause of domestic violence in many homes can be diverse as there are notably several causes of family dysfunction. A major cause of domestic violence can be frustration related to poverty and high rate of necessary unmet needs. In African theories, there are about five categories of explanation or theories of/to domestic violence. The five categories are namely: a.) Feminist theories b.) Rights theories, c.) Society-in-transition explanations, d.) Cultural explanations, e.) Cultural violence explanations. Until recently, domestic violence has always being viewed as a private marital matter. In the financial year of 2012, only one-third of the misconduct against women were reported and prosecuted in legal courts across Africa. Policies has been enacted to help increase the quality of life of those facing abuse and also to prevent continuous abuse. Domestic violence as defined by the 1998 Domestic violence act as the sexual abuse, physical abuse, verbal, psychological and emotional abuse, economic abuse, stalking, harassment, intimidation, damage to property, entry into complaint's home without the permission of the complainant or any other abusive or controlling attitude towards a complainant, to which such acts conducts imminent harms to the health, sanity, and safety of the complainant.

Domestic Violence against Women.

The level of violence against women is high and extremely alarming as it continues to have a demoralizing and long-term effect on victims. Also, it harms the families and communities across all age groups and constitutes one of the major factors of HIV in most African countries. In larger families in Africa, domestic violence is most prevalent as wives are constantly faced with emotional, psychological and sometimes physical abuse from their husband. Violence weakens socioeconomic development, it supports intergenerational phases of inequalities and poverty, its also obstructs the progress towards attaining the Millennium

Development goals as well as human rights realization. Domestic violence against women is never permissible or reasonable. Violence against women can be drastically reduced and in due course eliminated with the help of appropriate adequate resources and political will.

Presently, there is a significant gap between the daily violence experience faced by women and the international standards recognized by the national laws and policies. The issue now is to transform these standards into realism at the rural level to completely fight the problem from its root as well as the underlying causes with the essentially resources, accountability and political willingness. There is an imperative need for prompt national action to guard women and children from all types of violence. Prosecutors of violence should also be duly prosecuted and punished when apprehended to provide relief to victims. Approaches that are more strategic and cohesive is required so as to address the root and core causes of violence as well as reinforce the systems that responds to it.

The accurate degree of domestic violence against women cannot be fully measured as only small fractions are reported, investigated and prosecuted. However, there is liberal global and national evidence of its occurrence against women manifests in a continuous cycle and interrelated recurrent forms. Forms of women abuse may be include but not constrained to sexual harassment by partners, sexual violence, marital rape, domestic homicides, stalking and dangerous custom practices such as genital mutilation of the female reproductive organ and also forced early child marriages. Violence is experienced by women of all ages everyday in different forms and contexts. Sex trafficking and forced labour is a form of violence to which many developing African counties are forms to which women are travelled to different countries for sex work. Sex traffickers control their victims through intimidation, fear, debts bondage, forced use of addictive substances like hard drug and alcohol. Forms of violence against women are mostly from an informal face the woman knows and kept secret from family.

Domestic Violence against Children.

Millions of children grow up in societies that exposed them to violence from a tender age. The safety of the children is then compromised in the home as well as schools, community, justice and care systems. Exposure to violent acts in one form can influence another, for instance, in terms of life-threatening violence; there is a tendency to be high in family levels than school violence. Emotional, sexual and physical abuse and also bullying are parts of the typical forms of violence against children. This constitutes to low self-esteem of children and also negatively influences youthful exuberance of a teenager. In 2008, South Africa registered approximately 49,000 violent crimes against children. The role of media in exposing the level of violence against children and offering forms of battling violence is crucial.

Presently, children account for about 9% of most news stories in South Africa and other Sub-Saharan countries. When child abuse is televised or brought to the media, it rarely focuses on the cause but concentrates on the graphic details. Although the media carries advice and suggestions but there is an imperative need to influence prevention and reporting of the act to authorities. Media needs to be supported continually to make sure coverage of children to the highest moral standards to avert secondary trauma that may exist or happen as a result of immoral coverage. Unfortunately, perpetrators of violent acts of children are familiar faces such as friends, relatives, neighbour, and acquaintances that abuse takes place in their community. This result into the community of birth being unsafe for the child to lives, as it will continue to be a source of trauma and psychological disorder except adequate therapy and counselling is carried out on the child. For example, approximately one-third of parents or guardians reports using severe and inhumane types of corporal punishment against children.

In spite of the ban on corporal punishment in schools of most African countries, physical violence still widely occurs. A national research on school violence in South Africa conducted circa 2008, it was discovered that 15% of learners about 1.8 million kids experience some form of violence while in schools. These forms of punishment may include bullying by peers, humiliating type of punishment from tutors. In modern areas, gang acts also influence children's involvement in acts of violence. In Sub-Saharan African countries, for instance Kenya, Uganda, DRC, South Sudan, Nigeria, Togo and Niger, child labour is at its peak. Situations where children are not enrolled into schools but are sent to municipal areas of the country to work cheap labours and send the monthly wage for the upkeep of the family in rural areas. With this, the children are prone to violent acts mostly physically and sexually (if girls) by their bosses and treated unfairly most times. The long-term effects of these acts leave a demeaning effect on the confidence, self-worth, and self-esteem of the child.

CHAPTER 15

DOMESTIC VIOLENCE AGAINST MEN (WESTERN CONTEXT).

In Africa, domestic violence against men may seem unbelievable but not well expressed due to stigmatization. This chapter aims to promote the awareness that gender-based domestic violence is not only limited to women by men. Men are exposed to domestic violence in great numbers such as in the plight of couple violence, however they are less likely to hurt physically than females. Economically and socially disadvantaged groups in western countries like Australia and America often face worse degree of domestic violence. Violence against men comprises of violent deeds that are exclusively and unreasonably committed against men. The male gender is overrepresented as both perpetrator and victim of violence. Also, sexual violence against men is differently treated in any society from that committed against women also it may be unrecognized and unacknowledged by international law. Intimate Partner violence against men is concerned with involvements of domestic violence by boys or men in an intimate romantic relationship like dating, cohabitation, and marriage, within a family. Just as domestic violence against women constitutes crimes, it is also applicable in violence against men just that legislation varies between jurisdictions.

Although efforts have been made to promote female victims of domestic violence to report such acts to authority, there have been fairly few efforts to influence reporting to authorities by male victims. Men are faced with negative social stigma when they report acts of domestic violence against them. Such men are considered to lack chauvinism and other vilifications of their masculinity. In addition, intimate partner violence against men is less acknowledged generally by the society than intimate partner violence against females, therefore acts as a major obstacle to end reporting violent acts against them. The comparative dominance of intimate partner violence against men as compared to women is highly uncertain between several research conducted. Statistically, it is believed that the actual numbers of male victims may be greater but not documented due to the reluctance of male victims to report abuse. Domestic violence against man or woman is therefore considered as the least reported crime globally.

Gender symmetry, Bidirectional intimate partner violence and Battered Husband Syndrome are provocative areas of research, which contributes to a great deal of controversial debate. Typically, this line of debate tends to fall amid two fundamental arguments. It is argued that researchers who concentrate on female-enacted intimate partner violence are amongst the anti-feminist movement and are making efforts to destabilize the issue of domestic abuse by defending violence caused by men. The second argument argues that domestic violence against men is a crucial issue and underreported. Additionally, it puts women at risk of victimization by abusive men. Which radical feminist and scholars have overlooked so as to protect the basic gains of the abused women's campaign, especially the perspective that intimate partner maltreatment as an extension of male dominance. However, one of the tool used to collate statistics is argumentative, i.e. the Conflicts Tactic Scale.

Intimate partner violence is less recognized especially if the victims are men. Domestic violence against men perpetrated by women are mostly trivialized due to the hypothetical fragile physique of women, in cases as this, sharp dangerous objects and its use are omitted. Studies have identified problems of actual and perceived prejudice when security operatives are involved, with the male victim still stigmatized even whilst wounded physically or emotionally. Intimate partner violence or domestic violence occurs in heterosexual relationships and takes sexual, physical and emotional abuse as well as threats. Abusive relationships continuously involve disparity of control and power. Abusers used verbal, hurtful and intimidating words and attitudes to control their partner.

Recognizing domestic violence against men is not apparent or easily recognized, although traits of domestic acts may not be apparent early enough in a relationship as the behaviour is inherent and on the long-term it appears and the controlling and frightening features and the violence may occur as secluded incidents. Domestic violence in Africa is seriously undermined and trivialized, based on cultural norms and beliefs. Just as patriarchy is prevalent in most African countries, the discussion of domestic abuse of men are considered as weak discussions and forbidden as it ridicules the authority placed on patriarchy. Frustration, anguish, and continuous depression, are related to the psychiatric and psychological disorder to the man. Domestic violence against men can be seen as a form of reduced masculinity. Cultural and religious reasons also contribute to the lack of coming out of male victims of domestic violence. Family, friends and religious leaders will advise against reporting to authority, male ego and fear of embarrassment of household and colleagues will prompt the shunning off the idea reporting to the public. Traditionally, it is forbidden to see a man sober after being abused physically or emotionally by one's partner. Battered man ignores the call for help so as not to be seen as an incompetent man who cannot handle marital situations.

CHAPTER 16

AFRICAN PARENTAL ROLE: EARLY CHILD DEVELOPMENT, INVESTMENT, ENGAGEMENT AND EMPOWERMENT IN AUSTRALIAN CONTEXT.

The role of a parent is essential in the development and engagement is crucial as in an early childhood life. An African proverb states that "it takes a village to raise a child," therefore child development and empowerment is very crucial to the life of an African child. Children draw inspiration and strength from what they see their parents do, and the development and engagement of most children is mostly influenced by the ways of life of the parents. Parent involvement and parent engagement are frequently used interchangeably and when differentiated, the descriptions are most times not stable. From a grammar standpoint, parent involvement inclines to suggest what learning institutions are doing to parents i.e. informing parents exactly how to contribute, whilst parent engagement means to 'dong with' parents and achieving partnership in promoting child's overall development and education (Ferlazzo, 2009, 2011; Ferlazzo & Hammond, 2009).

Thus, the role of an African parent in the 'early' development of the child, empowerment, engagement and education in Australia is acknowledged as playing a major role in deciding the long term benefits and results all though the life of the child.

The development of the child's brain provides foundation for all future learning behaviour and promotes good health. In the first five years your child brain develops more quickly than any other age in their life. A child early experience is very crucial, what they see, hear, touch, smell and taste stimulates their brain and create connections with people and everything around them.

A close relationship between a child and a parent or caregiver is the best way to nourish the child growing brain, this happens through playing, singing, talking, storytelling, healthy feeding and above all love and affection, this helps the brain to developed and grow healthy. Being interactive with the child's life in safe and clean environment can make a big difference in a child growth development and future potentials.

Baby needs lots of care and affection in early years of growth, for instance, holding, cuddling and talking to stimulate the brain when a baby is kept close to the mother breastfed on demand, this provides the infant with a sense of emotional security. Baby crying is a way of communication, responding to the child crying by holding established a sense of trust and security. This type of bonding help the child to develop a broad range of ability to use throughout life, including ability to learn, self confidence, and have a positive social skills, have sympathy and eventually successful relationship at later age.

Both parents and family members need to be involved in caring and nurturing the growth, learning and development of children. Both boys and girls are equal. A father should make sure daughter and son feel equal and most importantly both parents should ensure that the children receives equal education and good nutrition and health care.

A major factor of quality early child development program is the excellent of relationship scholars develop with parents, guardians and families, therefore the relationship between parent involvement and engagement is not reciprocally exclusive to which educational institutions tend to go after both (Ferlazzo, 2009, 2011; Barton, Drake, Perez, Louis, & George, 2004). In most societies, Australia inclusive, disparities in the socioeconomic position translate into inequalities in child development (Goldfeld and West, 2014, Hertzman et al., 2010). Inconsistencies between children are centred on the preventive differences in economic and social conditions are obvious as early as 9 months in a variety of domains, and grow extensively over a period of time (Halle et al., 2009; Heckman, 2008).

The condition to which children are conceived into and exposed into is a determinant factor that influence or compromise healthy development of the child. The health, development and fitness of the children can be negotiated by several direct extreme experiences during and after pregnancy, which includes homelessness, family violence, drug abuse, parental alcohol, poverty, recurring neglect and abuse etc. The developments regarding the frequency of these issues in the African families living in Australia are disturbing (McDonald and Moore, 2013). This occurrence, is also apparent across a wide range of signs relating to families and children, results for families and children progressively improves the moving up of socioeconomic scale they are and deteriorate progressively the more down they move (Hertzman et al., 2010; Strategic Review of Health Inequalities in England post-2010 Committee, 2010). Therefore the poor kid and family results are not focused exclusively below the socioeconomic spectrum in a group of underprivileged families however distributed through the spectrum in a graded way (Wilkinson and Pickett, 2009; Denburg and Daneman, 2010).

Africans in a foreign country such as Australia should be well involved in the life of their progeny at the early stage of his or her life as this helps shape the mindset and influence decisions during the adolescent phase. Discriminations and social stigma due to native nationality may not be properly handle by the child in the early stage and therefore prone to bullying and negative peer pressure in terms of peer to peer interaction and social inclusion, hence the role of the African parent is crucial to help ease the process and overcome the deleterious effects. Encouraging relationship within home environment is essential for promoting the growth, development and learning of children. The quality of parent-to-child and or care-giver communication may be negotiated if the child has a physical or psychological disability. The involvement of both parents in the life of a child is critical especially in the early stage to 8 years of age. In most parts of the world, the relationship between parents and adolescent as well as provisions for the parent are under-developed. The impetus around parenting support is majorly for young children between ages 0 to 5years, although interventions for teenager's parents seem to be low particularly in the developing countries of Africa. However, there are few provisions made to cater for poor adolescent parents.

Supports and initiatives for parenting teenagers are discovered to be higher in volume is some developed countries like Netherlands and England to which the only type of parenting support if for the engagement and empowering of children at adolescent stages (Daly, 2013; Boddy et al., 2009). Customs round teenage mentoring by adults asides their birth parents are also noted foe countries such as Ireland and United States but not prevalent in Australia (Dolan and Brady, 2012). In a different place, initiatives and courses for parenting adolescents are infrequent and experimental in nature. Involvement of parents in the early childhood agendas has been associated with provision of rather high quality service (Cantin et al., 2012; Douglass, 2011; Elliott, 2003; Sylva et al., 2004. Operational partnerships between households and early years situations promote a more positive attitude towards the setting and establish a more durable connection for the young children who are vulnerable to experience less of a divide amid home and early years situation if family units and specialist respect and value one another (Fitzgerald, 2004).

Social barriers can contribute to the difficulty faced by African parents in Australia to be fully involved in the early development of their children. African parents from ethnic minorities are constantly faced with the challenges of accessing services (Jones et al., 2001). Cultural barriers have been identified to be related to the barriers African parents faced in the involvement of their children's development at an early stage (Barlow et al., 2004). Language and culture are peculiar constraints in the lifestyle of migrants in Australia, the school administration may take in that the parent is uninterested in the education of the child as a result of inability to commune fluently in English as well as the unavailability of a bilingual employee (Johnson, 2003). In Australia, refugee parents or migrants from minority ethnic groups may be from cultures where parents assume not to question or interfere or have interest in educational services nor child's education.

SUMMARY

This informative book has addressed diverse topics, causes, consequences, concepts, misconceptions that promotes poverty and unfairness to the female gender. Although Africa is rich in culture and natural resources, but it is constantly faced with issues like overpopulation and poverty. This resulted into several menaces that can hinder the progress of the continent and jeopardize the prospects of future generations. Explicitly and extensively discussed are consequences of continuous practice of polygyny, and its political and socioeconomic disadvantage to Africa, as well as how lack of quality education and basic social and care amenities has favoured the thriving of the epidemic HIV/AIDS in Africa. Also, the topic of intimate partner violence against women and men by heterosexual perpetrators as well as the discrimination and social stigma that comes with reporting to the prosecuting authority. The patriarchal culture of most countries in Africa influences the prevalence of gender inequality as well as gender expectations especially from the female child and promoting the demeaning act of early child marriage to which the defence argument is notably to prevent immoral decadence, prostitution and act as a ticket out of poverty for the household. Therefore, the need to put an end to larger families is imperative and African governments should support the sensitization into the local parts of Africa, the need for family planning and birth control measures, ensuring all myths and misconceptions are clearly debunked with actual facts. The governments should also duly fund poverty alleviation programs, particularly empowerment of women as the impact has a great positive potential to the advancement of socioeconomic development of most African countries.

References

1. Aneeza Pervez and Syeda Shahida Batool (2016). Polygamy: Chaos in the Relationships of Children. Pakistan Journal of Social and Clinical Psychology. Vol. 14, No.1, 30-35.

2. Adams, B. N., & Mburugu, E. (1994). Kikuyu bridewealth and POLYGAMY: CHAOS IN RELATIONSHIPS 34 polygyny today. Journal of Comparative Family Studies, 1, 159-166.

3. Al-Krenawi, A., Graham, J. R., & Al-Krenawi, S. (1997). Social work practice with polygamous families. Child and Adolescent Social Work Journal, 14(6), 445-458.

4. Jankowiak, W.R. (2008). Intimacies: Love and sex across cultures. New York, NY: Columbia University Press. Kilbride, P., & Kilbride, J. (1990). Changing family life in East Kenya: Women and children at risk. Philadelphia: University Park Press.

5. Elbedour, S., Onwuegbuzie, A. J., Caridine, C., & Abu-Saad, H. (2002). The effect of polygamous marital structure on behavioural,

emotional, and academic adjustment in children: A comprehensive review of the literature. Clinical Child and Family Psychology Review, 5(4), 255-271.

6. Mohammad Al-Sharfi, Karen Pfeffer and Kirsty A. Miller (2015). The effects of polygamy on children and adolescents: a systematic review. Journal of Family Studies. 1-28.

7. Shepard, L. D. (2013). The impact of polygamy on women's mental health: A systematic review. Epidemiology and psychiatric

sciences, 22, 47- 62.

8. Swanson, R. B., Masssey, R. H., & Payne, I. R. (1972). Ordinal position, family size, and personal adjustment. Journal of Psychology, 81, 51–58.

9. Owuamanam, D. O. (1984). Adolescents' perception of polygamous family and its relationship to self-concept. International Journal of Psychology, 19, 593-598.

10. Elbedour, S., Onwuegbuzie, A. J., Caridine, C., & Abu-Saad, H. (2002). The effect of polygamous

marital structure on behavioral, emotional, and academic adjustment in children: A comprehensive review of literature. Child and Family Psychology Review, 5(4), 555-271.

11. Chikwature W. and Oyedele V. (2016). Polygamy and Academic Achievement-A Case of Johanne Marange Apostolic Sect. European Journal of Research in Social Sciences, Vol. 4 No. 5.

12. https://www.huffingtonpost.com/diane-l-danois-jd/financial-infidelity-can-_b_3091991.html

13. https://www.cnbc.com/2014/02/07/more-spouses-are-cheating-financially-anyway.html

14. https://www.strongmarriagenow.com/warning-financial-dishonesty/

15. http://francisfinancial.com/the-impact-of-money-on-relationships/

16. http://www.un.org/africarenewal/magazine/july-2005/african-women-battle-equality

17. https://www.unicef.org/esaro/5481_girls_education.html

18. https://www.unicef.org/lifeskills/index_8657.html

19. https://www.theguardian.com/global-development/poverty-matters/2014/jul/22/child-marriage-gender-equality-girl-summit

20. http://www.ohchr.org/EN/NewsEvents/Pages/Childandforcedmarriagemanifestationofgenderdiscrimination.aspx

21. Wambua Leonard Munyao (2013). Gender Issues Affecting the Girl Child in Kenya. International Journal of Humanities and Social Science. Vol. 3 No. 4, 126-129pp.

22. https://blog.usaid.gov/2013/12/t

ransforming-gender-norms-and-
ending-child-marriage-the-role-of-
boys/

23. http://blogs.lse.ac.uk/africaatlse/
2013/10/23/the-cows-are-coming-
home-african-wedding-customs-
still-have-value-for-the-diaspora/

24. Theological Advisory Group
(1996). Payment of Dowry and the
Christian Church. Africa Journal of
Evangelical Theology 15 2. Pp 128-
134.

25. See South African Law
Commission, Project 90, The
Harmonization of the Common

Law and the Indigenous Law §
4.3.2.5 (Discussion Paper 74,
August 1997), at http://
www.law.wits.ac.za/salc/
discussn/dp74.html (last visited
August 4, 2004).

26. http://chora.virtualave.net/lobola
-hiv.htm

27. T.W. Bennett, Sourcebook of
African Customary Law 196-202
(1991).

28. South African Law
Commission, Project 90, The
Harmonization of the Common
Law and the Indigenous Law at §

4.3.2.6.

29. Bennett,supra at 202; South
African Law Commission, Project
90, The Harmonization of the
Common Law and the Indigenous
Law at § 4.3.2.6.

30. Winifred Brown, Marriage,
Divorce and Inheritance: The
Uganda Council of Women's
Movement for Legislative
Reform 54 (1988).

31. Mary Okioma , Bride price- Paving
The Way For A Killer, International
Conference on Bride Price and
Development February 2004

available at
http://www.mifumi.org/bp_confer ence/conference.htm

32. http:// www.unaids.org.

33. Vanessa von Struensee (2005). The Contribution of Polygamy to Women's Oppression and Impoverishment: An Argument for its Prohibition. Murdoch University Electronic Journal of Law. http://www5.austlii.edu.au/au/jour nals/MurUEJL/2005/2.html

34. Human Rights Watch, Double Standards: Women's Property Rights Violations in Kenya,

available at
http://www.hrw.org/reports/2003
/kenya0303/.

35. Human Rights Watch, Just Die
Quietly, supra.

36. Sedgh G and Hussain R, (2014).
Reasons for contraceptive nonuse
among women having unmet need
for contraception in developing
countries, Studies in Family
Planning, 45(2):151–169.

37. Paz Soldan VA, (2004) .How
family planning ideas are spread
within social groups in rural
Malawi, Studies in Family Planning,

35(4):275–290.

38. Yee L and Simon M, (2010). The role of the social network in contraceptive decision-making among young, African American and Latina women, Journal of Adolescent Health, 47(4):374–380.

39. Ankomah A, Anyanti J and Oladosu M, (2011). Myths, misinformation, and communication about family planning and contraceptive use in Nigeria, Open Access Journal of Contraception, 2(1):95–105.

40. DeClerque J et al., (1986). Rumor,

misinformation and oral contraceptive use in Egypt, Social Science & Medicine, 1986, 23(1):83–92.

41. Eliason S, Baiden F, Quansah-Asare G, Graham-Hayfron Y, Bonsu D, Phillips J, Awusabo-Asare K. Factors influencing the intention of women in rural Ghana to adopt postpartum family planning. Reprod Health [Online] 2013 Available from: http://www.ncbi.nlm.nih.gov/pmc/articles/PMC3724747/

42. Cates WJ, Abdool Karim Q, El-Sadr W, Haffner DW, Kalema-

Zikusoka G. (2010). Global development. Family planning and the millennium development goals. Science. \329:1603. [PubMed]

43. Sachs JD, McArthur JW. (2005). The millennium project: a plan for meeting the millennium development goals. Lancet. 365(9456):347–353. [PubMed]

44. Yue K, O'Donnel C, Sparks PL. (2010). The effect of spousal communication on contraceptive use in Central Terai, Nepal. Patient Educ Couns. 81(3):402–408. [PubMed]

45. Crossette B. (2005) Reproductive health and the millennium development goals: the missing link. Stud Fam Plann. 36:71–79. [PubMed]

46. Lauria L, Donati S, Spinelli A, Bonciani M, Grandolfo M. E. (2014).n The effect of contraceptive counselling in the pre and post-natal period on contraceptive use at three months after delivery among Italian and immigrant women. Ann Ist Super Sanita. 50(1):54–61. [PubMed]

47. Malini B, Narayanan E. (2014). Unmet need for family planning

among married women of
reproductive age group in urban
Tamil Nadu. Journal of Family &
Community Medicine. 21(1):53–5.
[PMC free article] [PubMed]

48. Kabagenyi A, Jennings L, Reid A,
Nalwadda G, Ntozi J, Atuyambe L.
(2014) Barriers to male involvement
in contraceptive uptake and
reproductive health services: a
qualitative study of men and
women's perceptions in two rural
districts in Uganda. Reprod. Health.
11(1):21. [PMC free article]
[PubMed]

49. Gaetano M, Lutuf A, Zaake D, Annika J. (2014). Predictors of Contraceptive use Among Female Adolescents in Ghana. Afr J Reprod Health March. 18 (1):102. [PubMed]

50. Odimegwu C. (2005) Influence of religion on adolescent sexual attitudes and behaviour among Nigerian University students: Affiliation or commitment? Afr J Reprod Health. 9(2):125–140.

51. https://assets.publishing.service.gov.uk/media/57a08967ed915d3cfd00021e/HDQ1249.pdf

52. DeRose, Laurie; Nii-Amoo Dodoo; Alex C. Ezeh; Tom O. Owuor (June 2004). "Does Discussion of Family Planning Improve Knowledge of Partner's Attitude Toward Contraceptives?

53. Gyimah, Stephen Obeng (June 2003). "A Cohort Analysis of the Timing of First Birth and Fertility in Ghana". Population Research and Policy Review. 22 (3): 251–266.

54. Alvergne, A; Lawson, D. W.; Clarke, P. M.R.; Gurmu, E.; Mace, R. (2013). "Fertility, parental investment, and the early adoption

of modern contraception in rural ethiopia". American Journal of Human Biology. 25: 107–115. doi:10.1002/ajhb.22348

55. "Family planning". World Health Organization. 2012

56. https://www.economist.com/news/middle-east-and-africa/21721325-faith-and-tradition-favour-high-fertility-education-pulls-other-way

57. http://journals.sagepub.com/doi/abs/10.1177/0272684X16685254

58. Rutenberg, N; Watkins SC (Oct 1997). "The buzz outside the

clinics: conversations and contraception in Nyanza Province, Kenya". Stud Fam Plann. 28: 290–307.

59. Rhoune Ochako, corresponding author Mwende Mbondo, Stephen Aloo, Susan Kaimenyi, Rachel Thompson, Marleen Temmerman, and Megan Kays (2015). Barriers to modern contraceptive methods uptake among young women in Kenya: a qualitative study. BMC Public Health v.15; 2015.

60. https://assets.publishing.service.g ov.uk/media/57a08967ed915d3cfd

61. Rikhotso, M., Namumba, L., Morwe, K. and Dibetso, L. (2013) Promoting Children's Rights: Coverage of Children in South African and Zambian Media.

62. Dawes, A., De Sas Kropiwnicki, Z., Kafaar, Z. and Richter, L. (2005) Corporal Punishment of Children: A South African National Survey.

63. Burton, P. (2008) Merchants, Skollies and Stones: Experiences of School Violence in South Africa.

64. Norman R., Schneider M.,

Bradshaw D., Jewkes R., Abrahams N., Matzopoulos R. and Vos T. (2010) Interpersonal Violence: An Important Risk Factor for Disease and Injury in South Africa.

65. http://www.dsd.gov.za/index2.php?option=com_docman&task=doc_view&gid=607&Itemid=

66. Young, Cathy (June 25, 2014). "The surprising truth about women and violence". TIME. Retrieved February 24, 2015.

67. http://www.scielo.org.za/scielo.php?script=sci_arttext&pid=S0259-

94222015000100014

68. https://www.mheducation.co.uk/openup/chapters/9780335212484.pdf

69. Goldfeld S. West S. (2014) Inequalities in Early Childhood Outcomes: What Lies Beneath. Insight Issue 9. Victorian Council of Social Services (VCOSS), Melbourne, Australia.

70. Hertzman C. Siddiqi A. Hertzman E. Irwin L. G. Vaghri Z. Houweling T. A. J.et al. (2010) Bucking the inequality gradient through early child development. British Medical

Journal, 340, c468.

71. Halle T. Forry N. Hair E. Perper K. Wandner L. Wessel J. Vick J. (2009) Disparities in Early Learning and Development: Lessons from the Early Childhood Longitudinal Study – Birth Cohort (ECLS-B). Child Trends, Washington, DC.

72. Heckman J. J. (2008) Schools, skills, and synapses (NBER Working Paper 14064). National Bureau of Economic Research, Cambridge, Massachusetts.

73. Denburg A. Daneman D. (2010). The link between social inequality

and child health outcomes.
Healthcare Quarterly, 14(Sp), 21–
31.

74. Moore T. G. McDonald M. (2013)
Acting Early, Changing Lives: How
Prevention and Early Action Saves
Money and Improves Wellbeing.
The Benevolent Society,
Paddington, Australia.

75. Wilkinson R. G. Pickett K. E.
(2009) The Sprit Level: Why More
Equal Societies Almost Always Do
Better. Allen Lane, London, UK.

76. Children with disabilities: ending
discrimination and promoting

participation, development, and inclusion. New York, United Nations Children's Fund, 2007.

77. Promoting the rights of children with disabilities (Innocenti Digest No. 13). Florence, United Nations Children's Fund, Innocenti Research Centre, 2007.

78. World Health Organization, World Bank. World report on disability. Geneva, World Health Organization, 2011. http://www.who.int/disabilities/world_report/2011/en/index.html

79. Jones, L., Atkin, K. and Ahmad,

W. (2001) 'Supporting Asian deaf young people and their families: the role of professionals and services', Disability and Society, Vol. 16, No. 1, pp. 51–70

80. Barlow, J., Shaw, R. and Stewart Brown, S. in conjunction with REU (2004) Parenting Programmes and Minority Ethnic Families: Experiences and Outcomes. London: National Children's Bureau

81. Johnson, S. (2003) Involving Immigrant and Refugee Families in their Children's Schools: Barriers, Challenges and Successful

Strategies. http://www.isbe.net/
bilingual/pdfs/involving_families.p
df

82. Ferlazzo, L. (2009). Parent
Involvement or Parent
Engagement?. Learning First
Alliance: Strengthening public
schools for every child. Retrieved
from
http://www.learningfirst.org/Larry
FerlazzoParentEngagement.

83. Ferlazzo, L. (2011). Involvement
or engagement? Educational
Leadership, 68(8), 10–14.

84. Ferlazzo, L., & Hammond, L. A.

(2009). Building Parent Engagement in Schools. Santa Barbara, CA: Linworth Publishing.

85. Sylva K. Melhuish E. Sammons P. Siraj-Blatchford I. Taggart B. Elliot K. (2003) The Effective Provision of Pre-School Education (EPPE) Project. Findings from the Preschool Period (Research Brief, Brief No. RBX 15-03). Institute of Education, University of London, University of Oxford and Birkbeck, University of London, London, UK.

86. https://thisisafrica.me/pill-friend-10-debunked-myths-oral-

contraceptives/

www.ingramcontent.com/pod-product-compliance
Lightning Source LLC
Chambersburg PA
CBHW060801050426
42449CB00008B/1474